# HAZEL NEWLEVANT

# SUGAR TOWN

For the real
Gregor and Argent

ISBN  978-1-68148-587-4

Printed in the United States

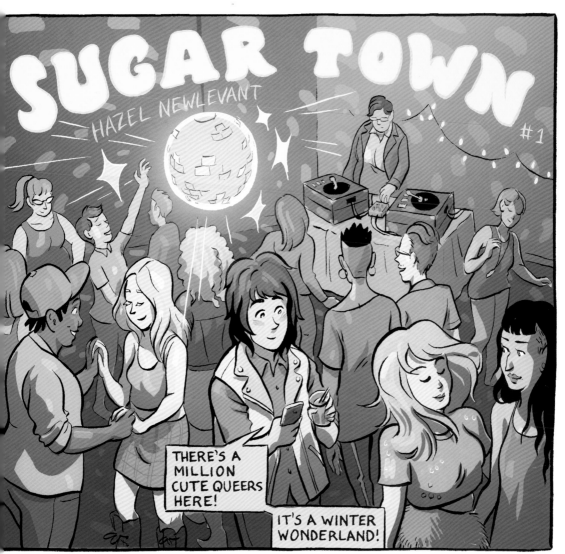

# SUGAR TOWN

HAZEL NEWLEVANT

#1

THERE'S A MILLION CUTE QUEERS HERE!

IT'S A WINTER WONDERLAND!

AND I'M THE WEIRD ELF WHO DOESN'T KNOW ANY— ONE.

sluurp

Gregor:

DOESN'T MEAN YOU CAN'T HAVE A GOOD TIME!

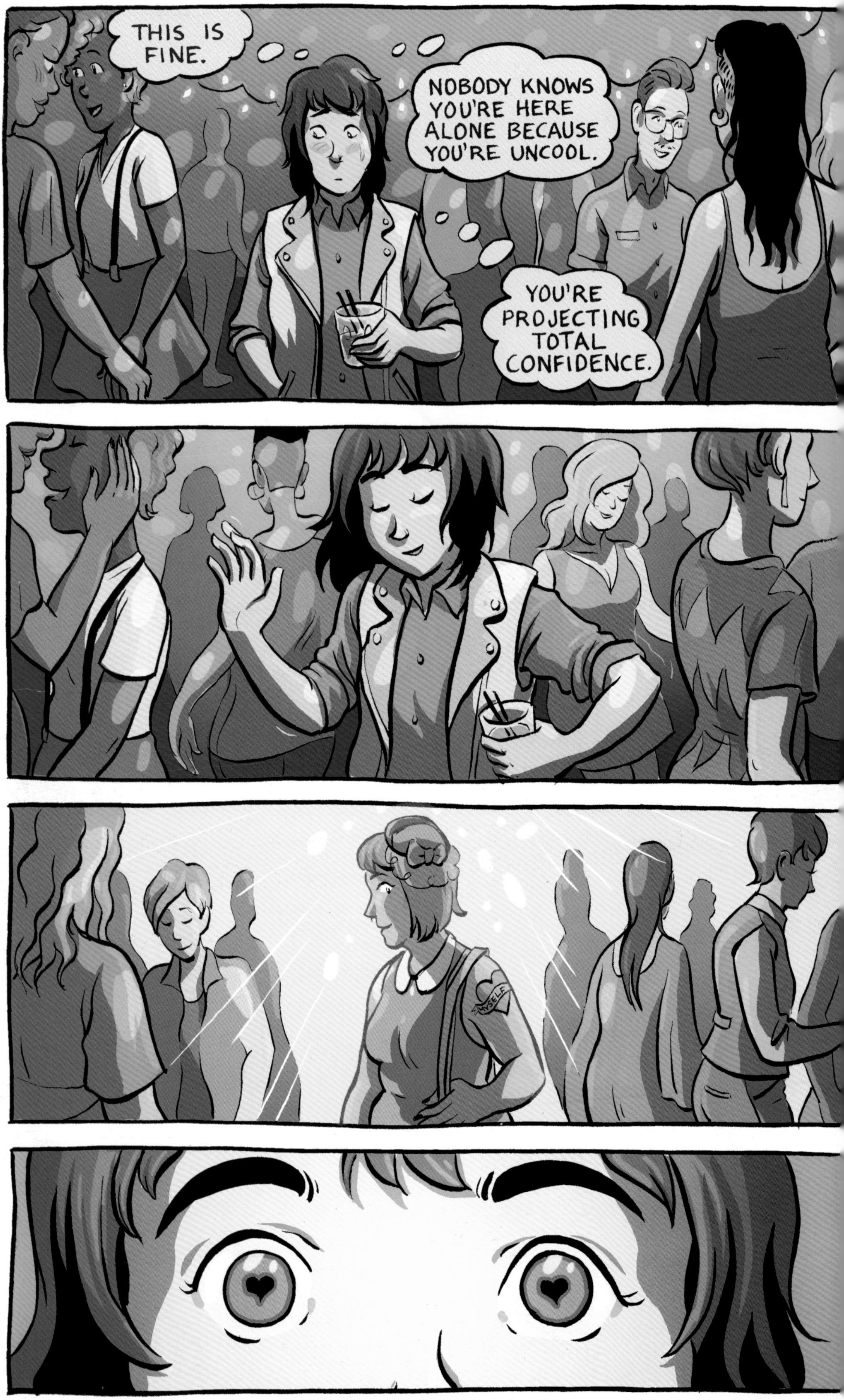
THIS IS FINE.
NOBODY KNOWS YOU'RE HERE ALONE BECAUSE YOU'RE UNCOOL.
YOU'RE PROJECTING TOTAL CONFIDENCE.
MYSELF

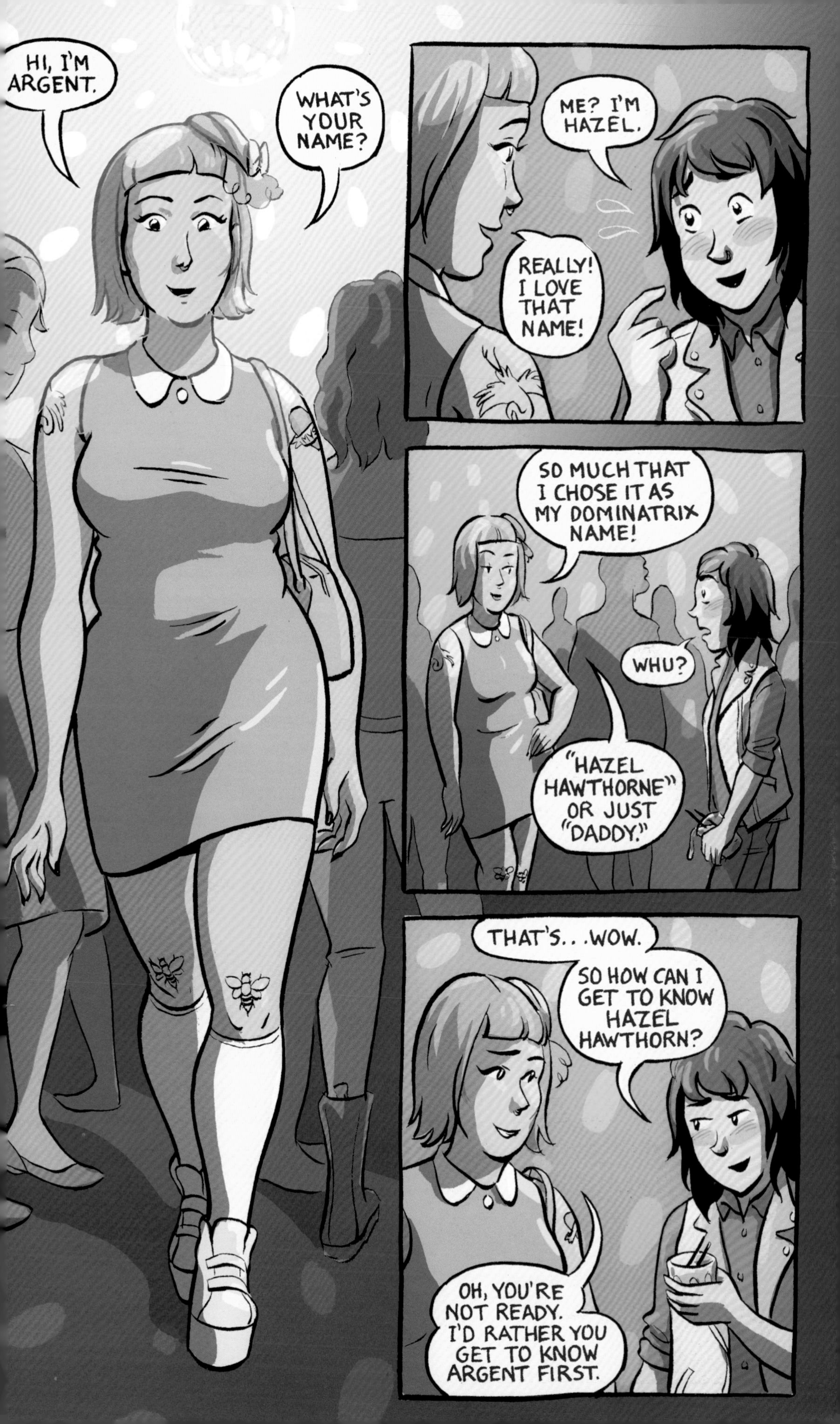
HI, I'M ARGENT.
WHAT'S YOUR NAME?
ME? I'M HAZEL.
REALLY! I LOVE THAT NAME!
SO MUCH THAT I CHOSE IT AS MY DOMINATRIX NAME!
WHU?
"HAZEL HAWTHORNE" OR JUST "DADDY."
THAT'S. . .WOW.
SO HOW CAN I GET TO KNOW HAZEL HAWTHORN?
OH, YOU'RE NOT READY. I'D RATHER YOU GET TO KNOW ARGENT FIRST.

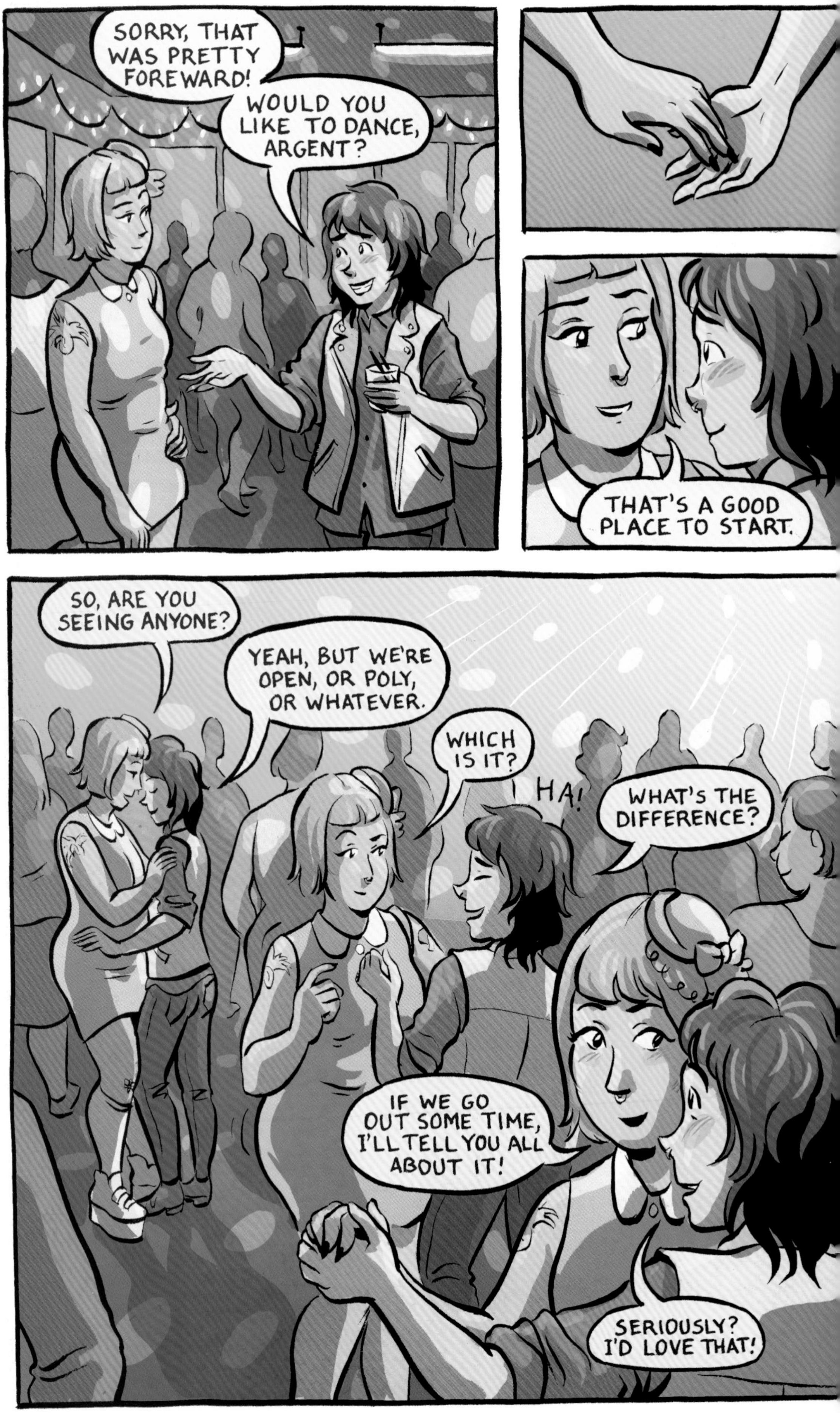
SORRY, THAT WAS PRETTY FOREWARD!
WOULD YOU LIKE TO DANCE, ARGENT?
THAT'S A GOOD PLACE TO START.
SO, ARE YOU SEEING ANYONE?
YEAH, BUT WE'RE OPEN, OR POLY, OR WHATEVER.
WHICH IS IT?
HA!
WHAT'S THE DIFFERENCE?
IF WE GO OUT SOME TIME, I'LL TELL YOU ALL ABOUT IT!
SERIOUSLY? I'D LOVE THAT!

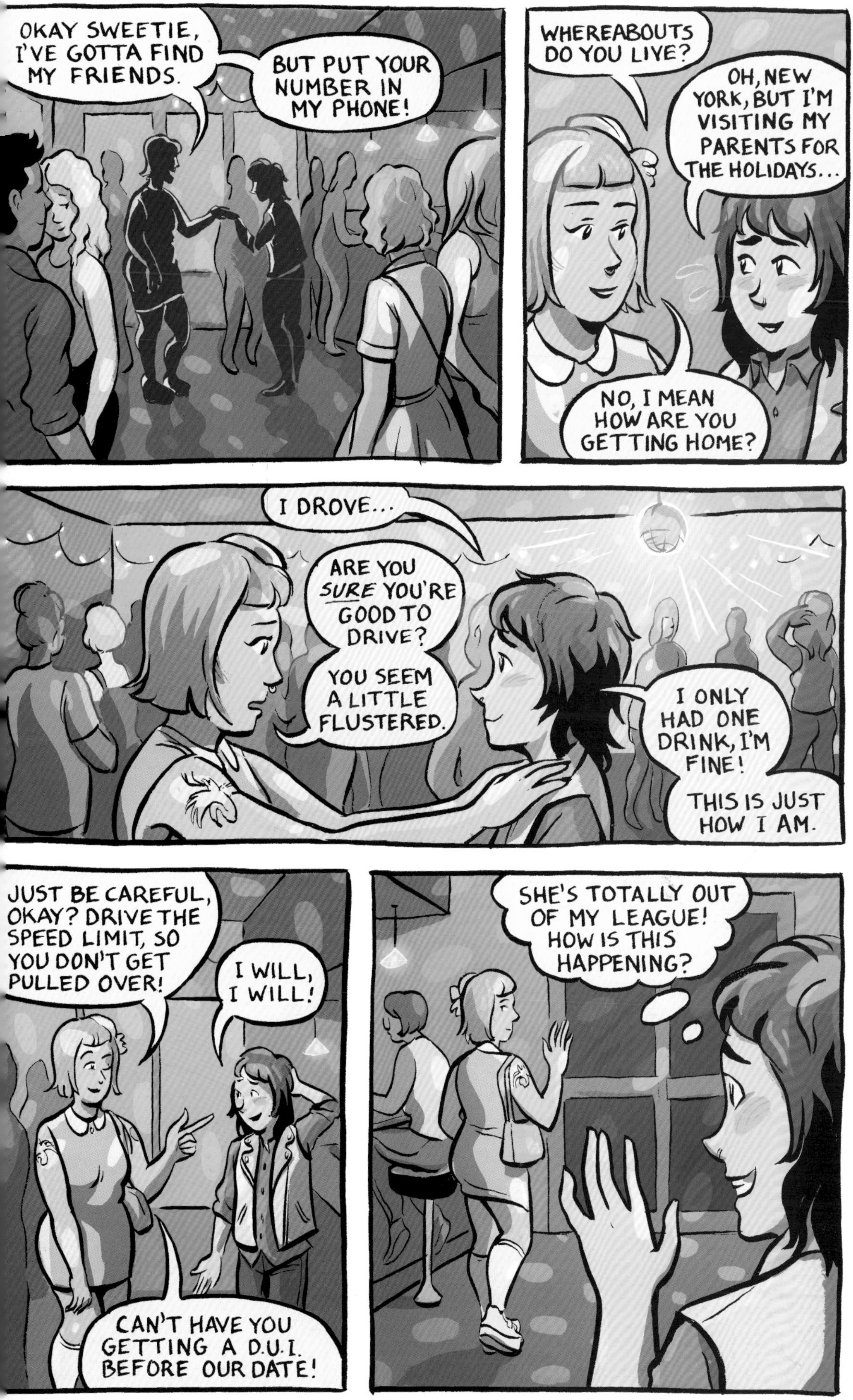
OKAY SWEETIE, I'VE GOTTA FIND MY FRIENDS.
BUT PUT YOUR NUMBER IN MY PHONE!
WHEREABOUTS DO YOU LIVE?
OH, NEW YORK, BUT I'M VISITING MY PARENTS FOR THE HOLIDAYS...
NO, I MEAN HOW ARE YOU GETTING HOME?
I DROVE...
ARE YOU SURE YOU'RE GOOD TO DRIVE?
YOU SEEM A LITTLE FLUSTERED.
I ONLY HAD ONE DRINK, I'M FINE!
THIS IS JUST HOW I AM.
JUST BE CAREFUL, OKAY? DRIVE THE SPEED LIMIT, SO YOU DON'T GET PULLED OVER!
I WILL, I WILL!
CAN'T HAVE YOU GETTING A D.U.I. BEFORE OUR DATE!
SHE'S TOTALLY OUT OF MY LEAGUE! HOW IS THIS HAPPENING?

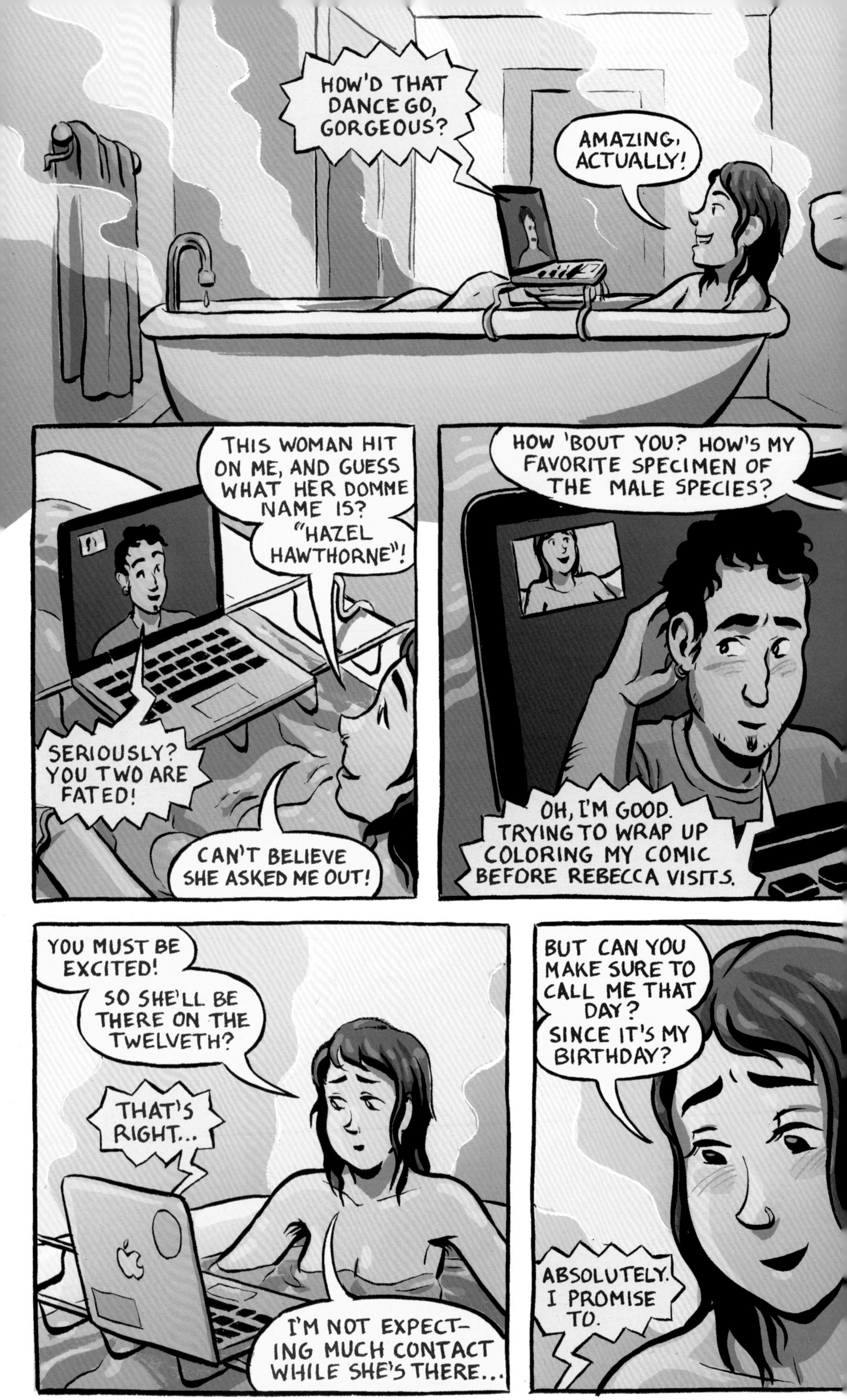
HOW'D THAT DANCE GO, GORGEOUS?
AMAZING, ACTUALLY!
THIS WOMAN HIT ON ME, AND GUESS WHAT HER DOMME NAME IS? "HAZEL HAWTHORNE"!
SERIOUSLY? YOU TWO ARE FATED!
CAN'T BELIEVE SHE ASKED ME OUT!
HOW 'BOUT YOU? HOW'S MY FAVORITE SPECIMEN OF THE MALE SPECIES?
OH, I'M GOOD. TRYING TO WRAP UP COLORING MY COMIC BEFORE REBECCA VISITS.
YOU MUST BE EXCITED!
SO SHE'LL BE THERE ON THE TWELVETH?
THAT'S RIGHT...
I'M NOT EXPECT-ING MUCH CONTACT WHILE SHE'S THERE...
BUT CAN YOU MAKE SURE TO CALL ME THAT DAY? SINCE IT'S MY BIRTHDAY?
ABSOLUTELY. I PROMISE TO.

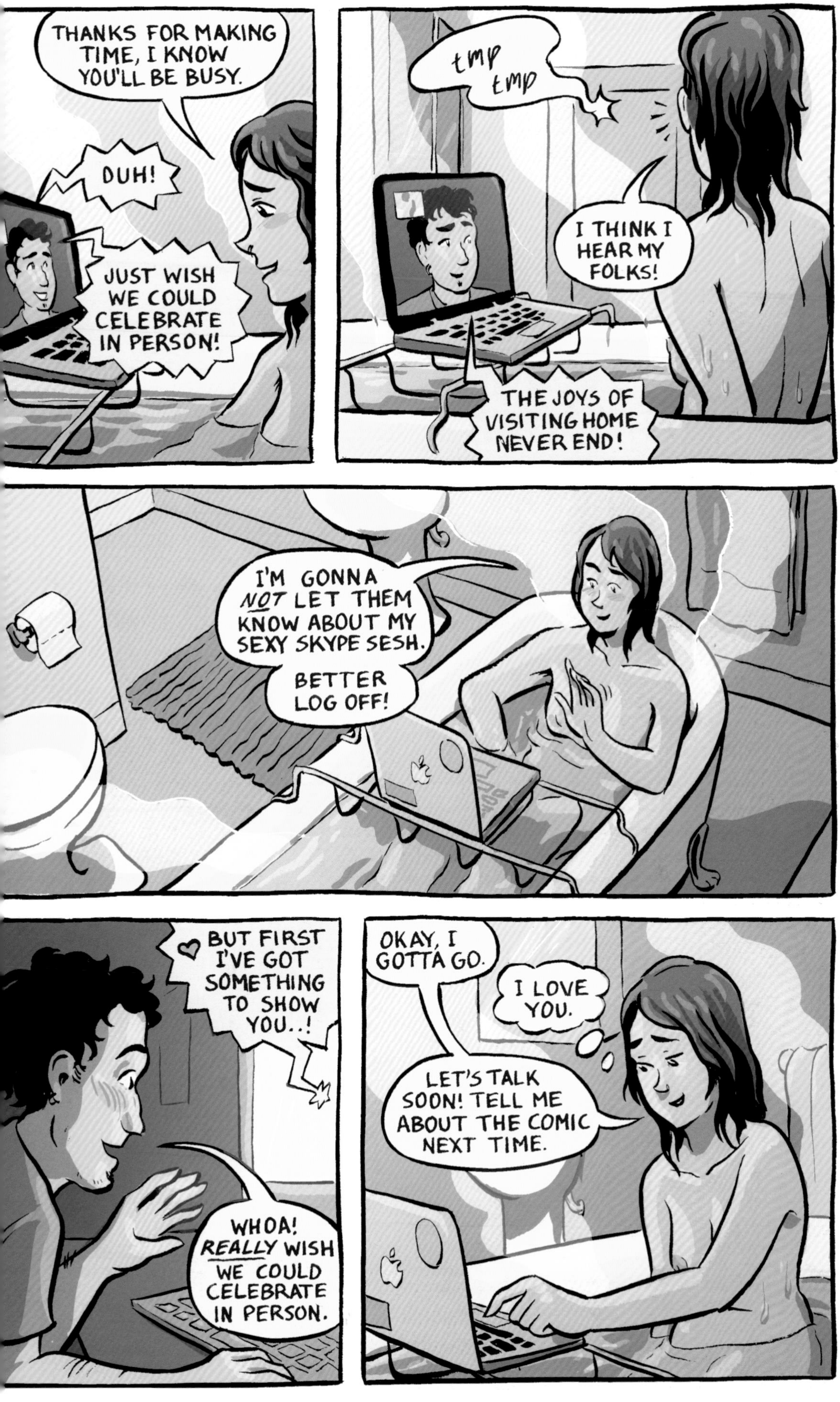
THANKS FOR MAKING TIME, I KNOW YOU'LL BE BUSY.
DUH!
JUST WISH WE COULD CELEBRATE IN PERSON!
tmp tmp
I THINK I HEAR MY FOLKS!
THE JOYS OF VISITING HOME NEVER END!
I'M GONNA NOT LET THEM KNOW ABOUT MY SEXY SKYPE SESH.
BETTER LOG OFF!
BUT FIRST I'VE GOT SOMETHING TO SHOW YOU..!
WHOA! REALLY WISH WE COULD CELEBRATE IN PERSON.
OKAY, I GOTTA GO.
I LOVE YOU.
LET'S TALK SOON! TELL ME ABOUT THE COMIC NEXT TIME.

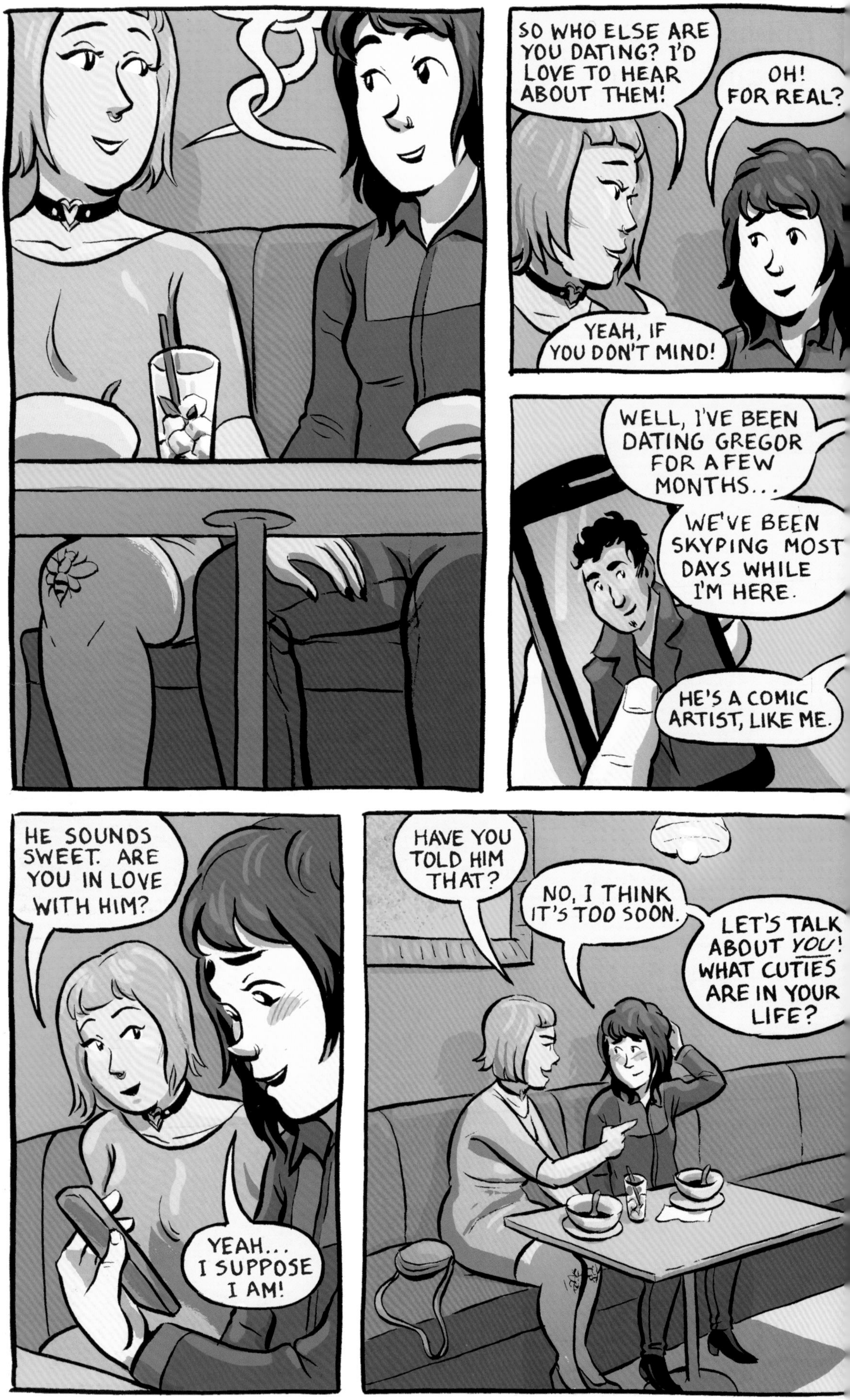
SO WHO ELSE ARE YOU DATING? I'D LOVE TO HEAR ABOUT THEM!
OH! FOR REAL?
YEAH, IF YOU DON'T MIND!
WELL, I'VE BEEN DATING GREGOR FOR A FEW MONTHS...
WE'VE BEEN SKYPING MOST DAYS WHILE I'M HERE.
HE'S A COMIC ARTIST, LIKE ME.
HE SOUNDS SWEET. ARE YOU IN LOVE WITH HIM?
YEAH... I SUPPOSE I AM!
HAVE YOU TOLD HIM THAT?
NO, I THINK IT'S TOO SOON.
LET'S TALK ABOUT YOU! WHAT CUTIES ARE IN YOUR LIFE?

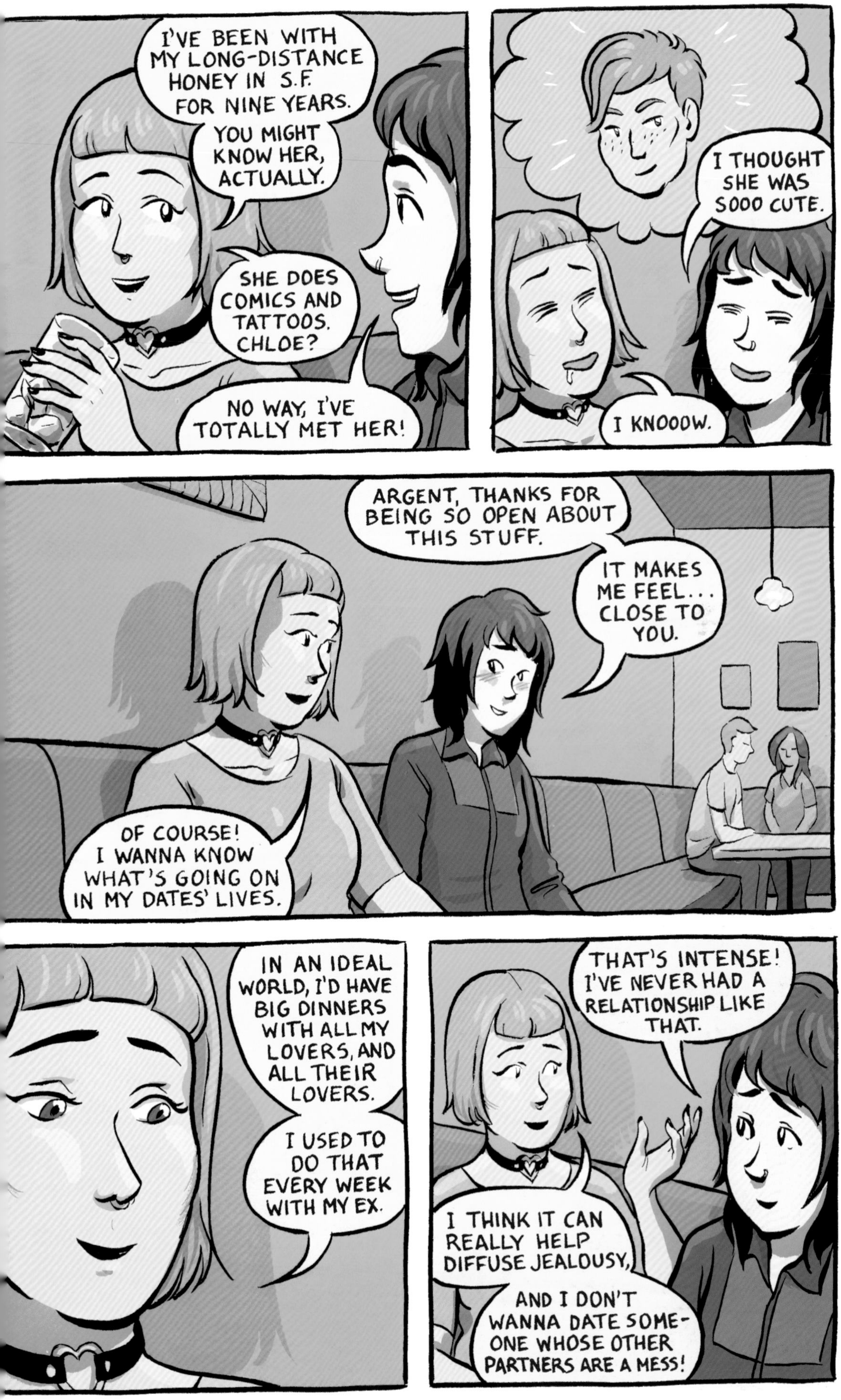
I'VE BEEN WITH MY LONG-DISTANCE HONEY IN S.F. FOR NINE YEARS.
YOU MIGHT KNOW HER, ACTUALLY.
SHE DOES COMICS AND TATTOOS. CHLOE?
NO WAY, I'VE TOTALLY MET HER!
I THOUGHT SHE WAS SOOO CUTE.
I KNOOOW.
ARGENT, THANKS FOR BEING SO OPEN ABOUT THIS STUFF.
IT MAKES ME FEEL... CLOSE TO YOU.
OF COURSE! I WANNA KNOW WHAT'S GOING ON IN MY DATES' LIVES.
IN AN IDEAL WORLD, I'D HAVE BIG DINNERS WITH ALL MY LOVERS, AND ALL THEIR LOVERS.
I USED TO DO THAT EVERY WEEK WITH MY EX.
THAT'S INTENSE! I'VE NEVER HAD A RELATIONSHIP LIKE THAT.
I THINK IT CAN REALLY HELP DIFFUSE JEALOUSY,
AND I DON'T WANNA DATE SOME-ONE WHOSE OTHER PARTNERS ARE A MESS!

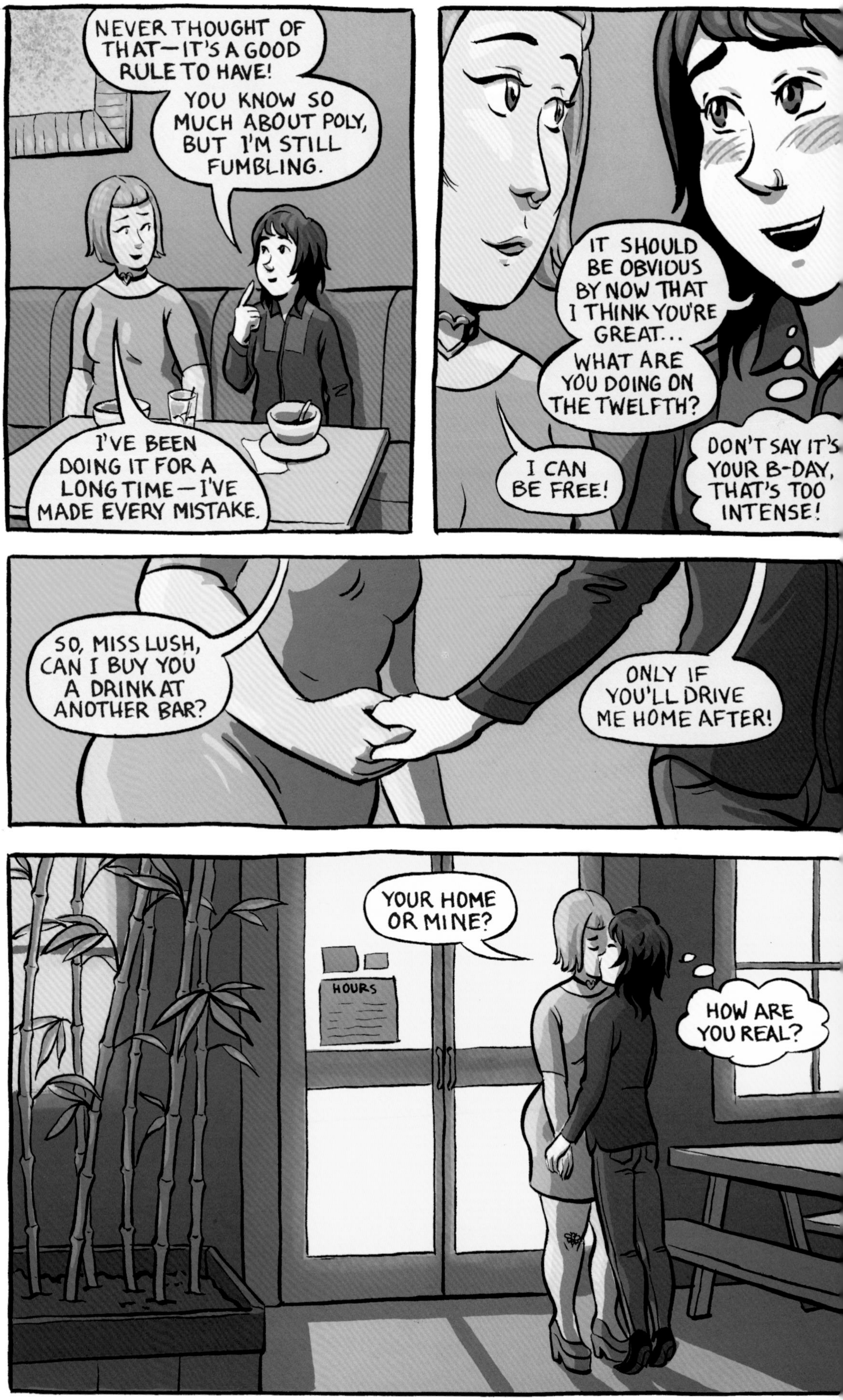
NEVER THOUGHT OF THAT—IT'S A GOOD RULE TO HAVE!
YOU KNOW SO MUCH ABOUT POLY, BUT I'M STILL FUMBLING.
I'VE BEEN DOING IT FOR A LONG TIME—I'VE MADE EVERY MISTAKE.
IT SHOULD BE OBVIOUS BY NOW THAT I THINK YOU'RE GREAT...
WHAT ARE YOU DOING ON THE TWELFTH?
I CAN BE FREE!
DON'T SAY IT'S YOUR B-DAY, THAT'S TOO INTENSE!
SO, MISS LUSH, CAN I BUY YOU A DRINK AT ANOTHER BAR?
ONLY IF YOU'LL DRIVE ME HOME AFTER!
YOUR HOME OR MINE?
HOURS
HOW ARE YOU REAL?

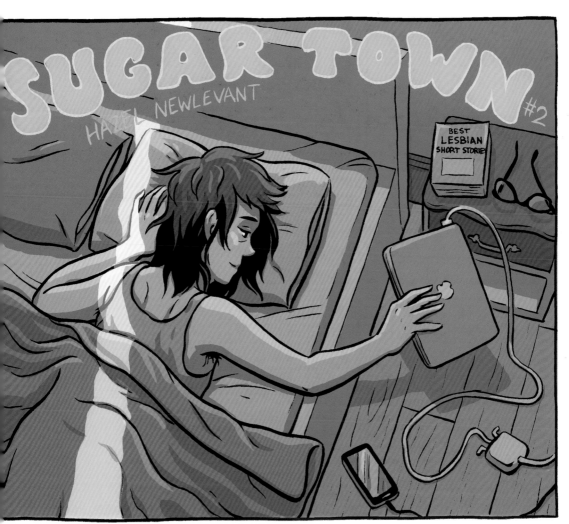

SUGAR TOWN

HAZEL NEWLEVANT

#2

BEST LESBIAN SHORT STORIES

Pete Dawgkins ▸ Haze
20 mins

hap b day, i hope u play magic with some1 hot.

Like        💬 Comment

Write a comment...

Jamie the Juicer ▸ Haze
2 hrs

Happy birthday, ya old fart
😊◁³

NOT WHO I *REALLY* WANTED TO HEAR FROM...

GUESS HE'S BUSY WITH HIS OTHER LADY.

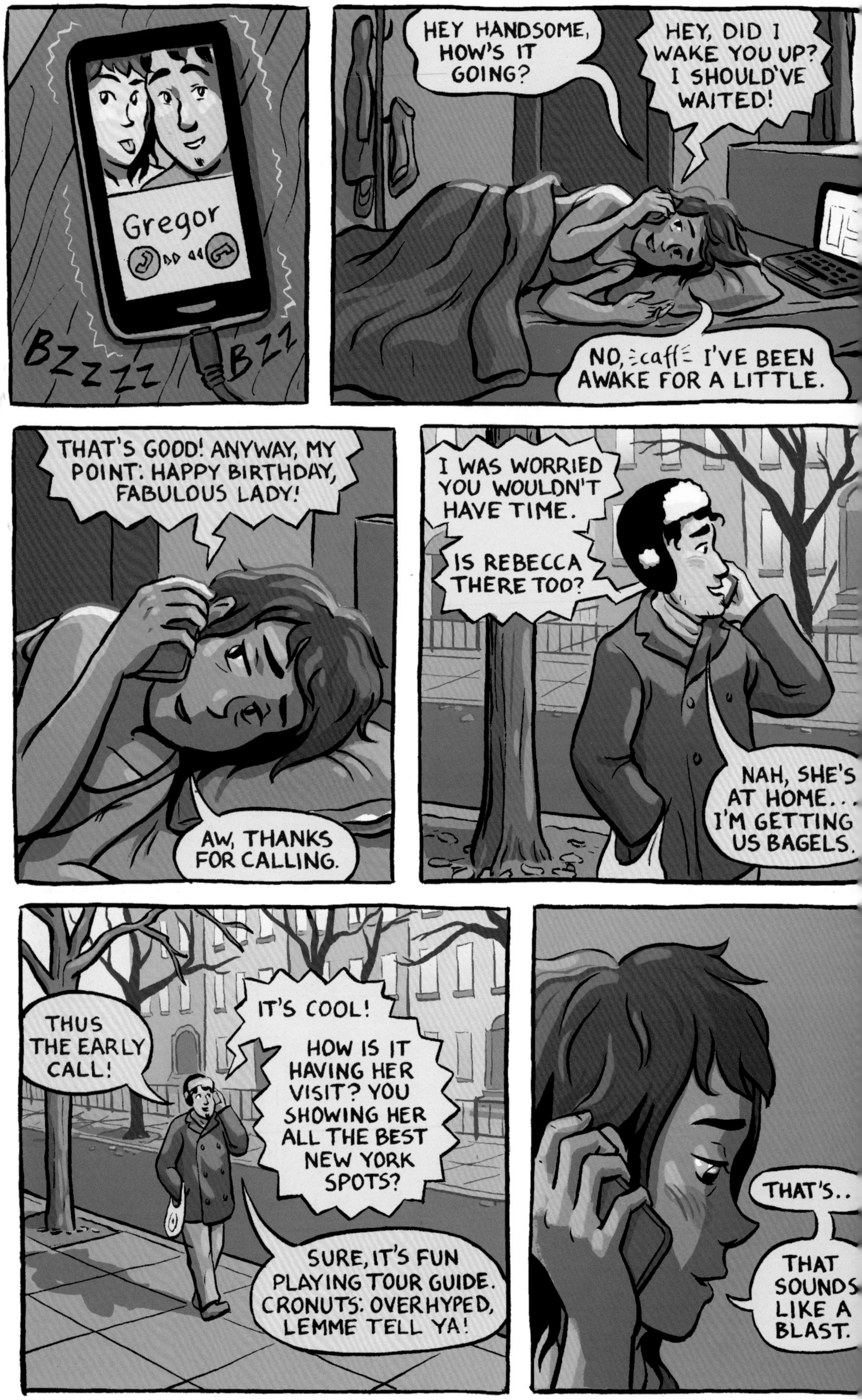
Gregor
BZZZZZ BZZ
HEY HANDSOME, HOW'S IT GOING?
HEY, DID I WAKE YOU UP? I SHOULD'VE WAITED!
NO, cough I'VE BEEN AWAKE FOR A LITTLE.
THAT'S GOOD! ANYWAY, MY POINT: HAPPY BIRTHDAY, FABULOUS LADY!
AW, THANKS FOR CALLING.
I WAS WORRIED YOU WOULDN'T HAVE TIME.
IS REBECCA THERE TOO?
NAH, SHE'S AT HOME... I'M GETTING US BAGELS.
THUS THE EARLY CALL!
IT'S COOL!
HOW IS IT HAVING HER VISIT? YOU SHOWING HER ALL THE BEST NEW YORK SPOTS?
SURE, IT'S FUN PLAYING TOUR GUIDE. CRONUTS: OVERHYPED, LEMME TELL YA!
THAT'S..
THAT SOUNDS LIKE A BLAST.

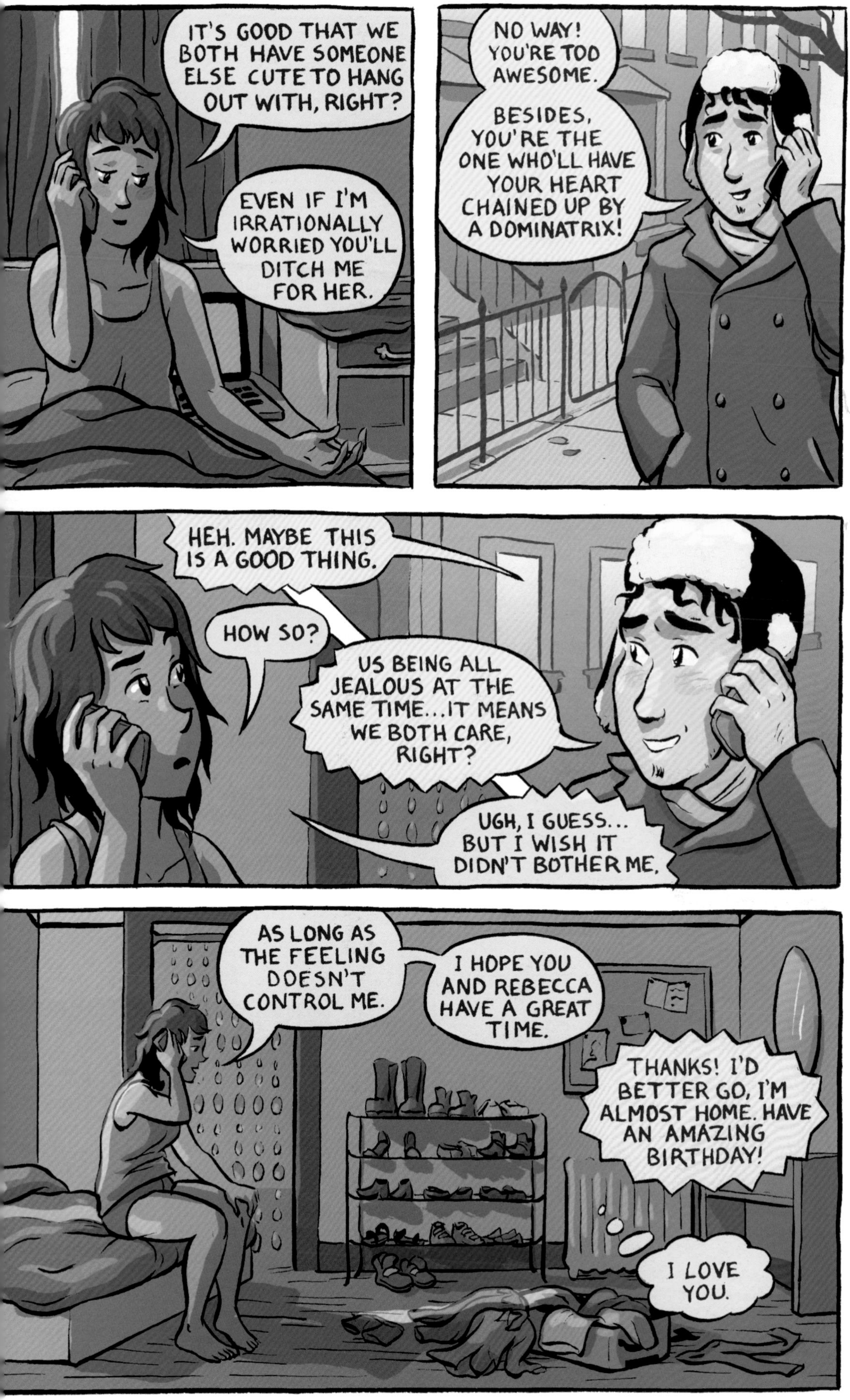
IT'S GOOD THAT WE BOTH HAVE SOMEONE ELSE CUTE TO HANG OUT WITH, RIGHT?
EVEN IF I'M IRRATIONALLY WORRIED YOU'LL DITCH ME FOR HER.
NO WAY! YOU'RE TOO AWESOME.
BESIDES, YOU'RE THE ONE WHO'LL HAVE YOUR HEART CHAINED UP BY A DOMINATRIX!
HEH. MAYBE THIS IS A GOOD THING.
HOW SO?
US BEING ALL JEALOUS AT THE SAME TIME...IT MEANS WE BOTH CARE, RIGHT?
UGH, I GUESS... BUT I WISH IT DIDN'T BOTHER ME.
AS LONG AS THE FEELING DOESN'T CONTROL ME.
I HOPE YOU AND REBECCA HAVE A GREAT TIME.
THANKS! I'D BETTER GO, I'M ALMOST HOME. HAVE AN AMAZING BIRTHDAY!
I LOVE YOU.

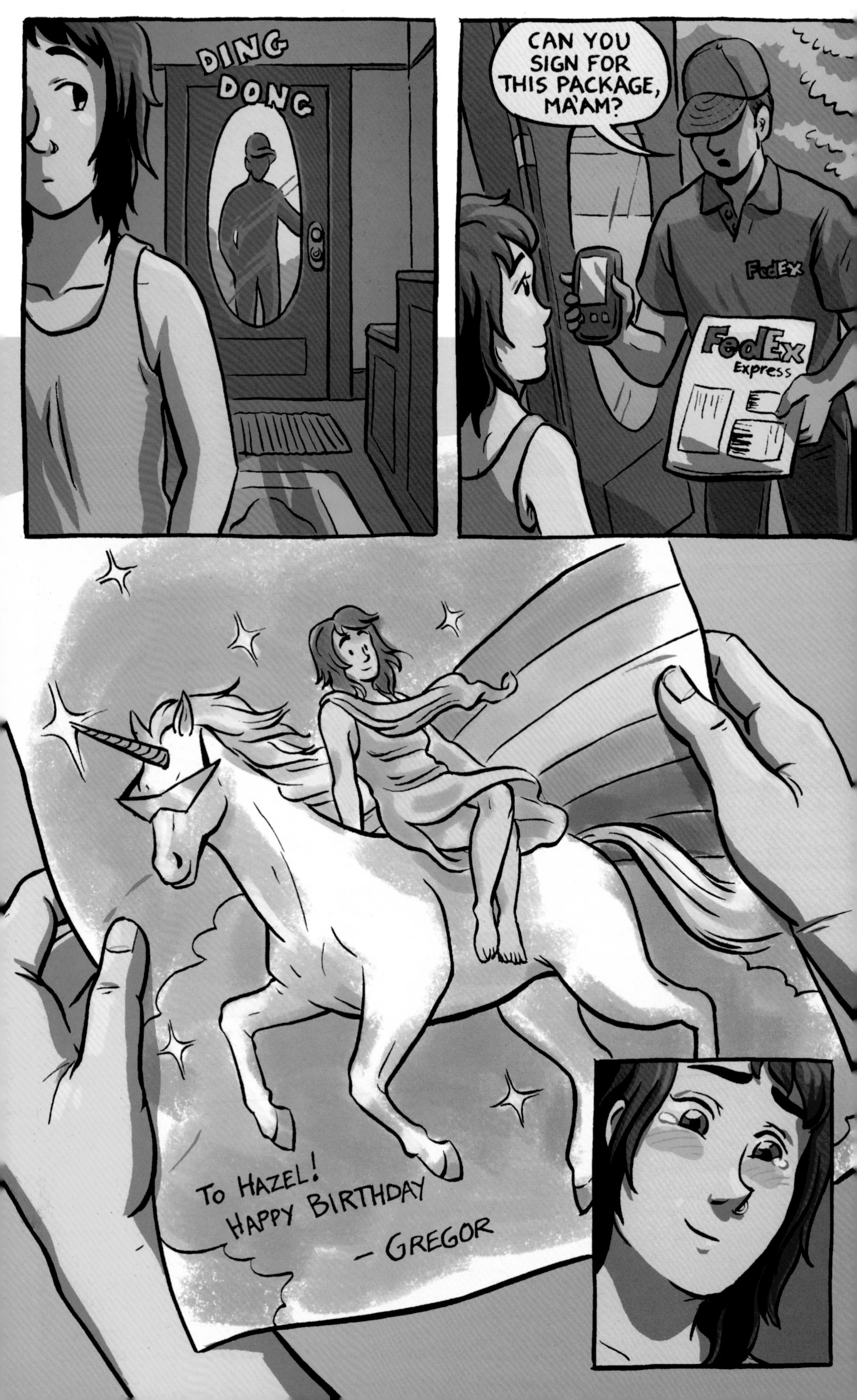
DING DONG
CAN YOU SIGN FOR THIS PACKAGE, MA'AM?
FedEx
FedEx Express
To Hazel! Happy Birthday
- Gregor

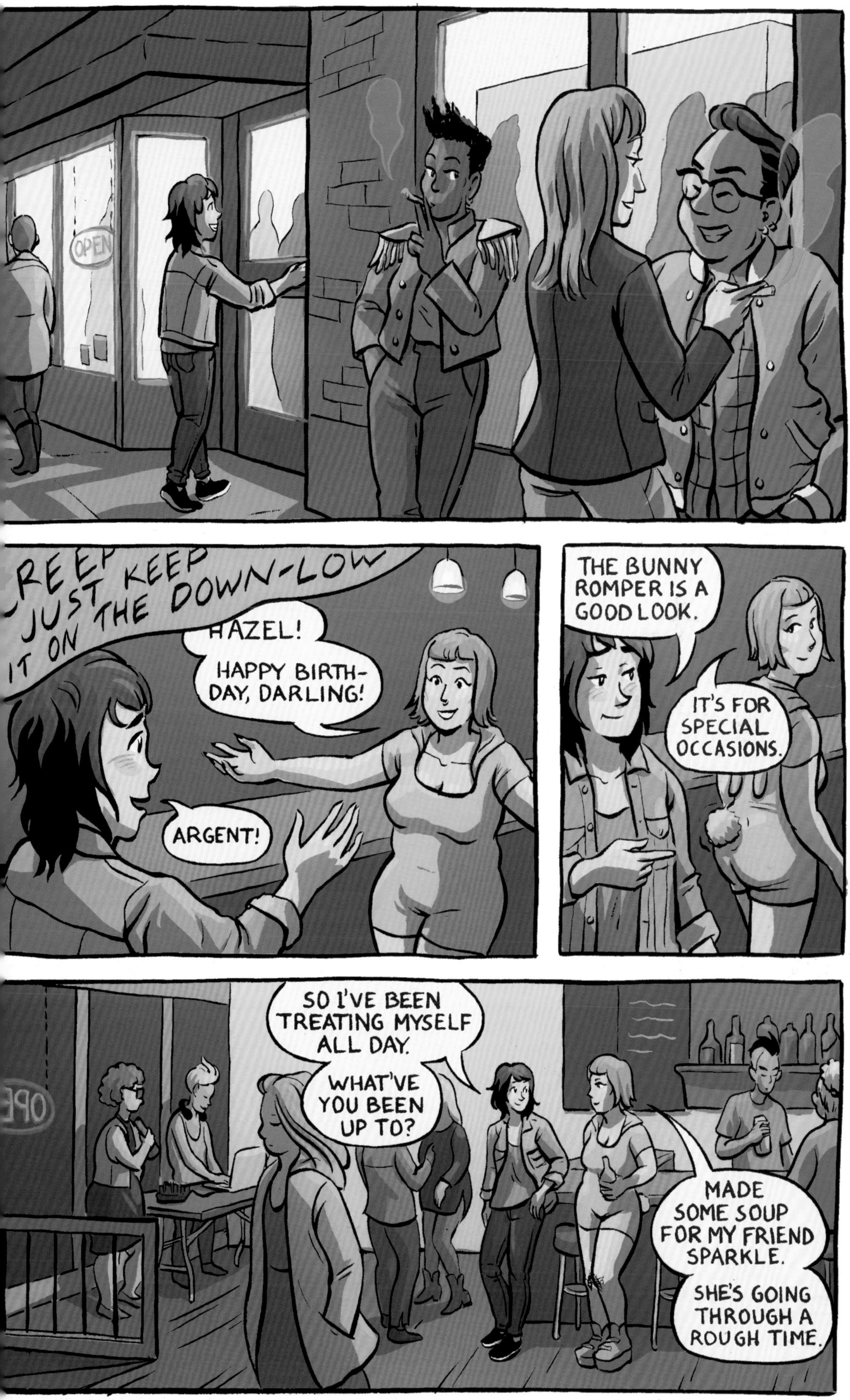

JUST KEEP IT ON THE DOWN-LOW
HAZEL!
HAPPY BIRTH-DAY, DARLING!
ARGENT!
THE BUNNY ROMPER IS A GOOD LOOK.
IT'S FOR SPECIAL OCCASIONS.
SO I'VE BEEN TREATING MYSELF ALL DAY.
WHAT'VE YOU BEEN UP TO?
MADE SOME SOUP FOR MY FRIEND SPARKLE.
SHE'S GOING THROUGH A ROUGH TIME.

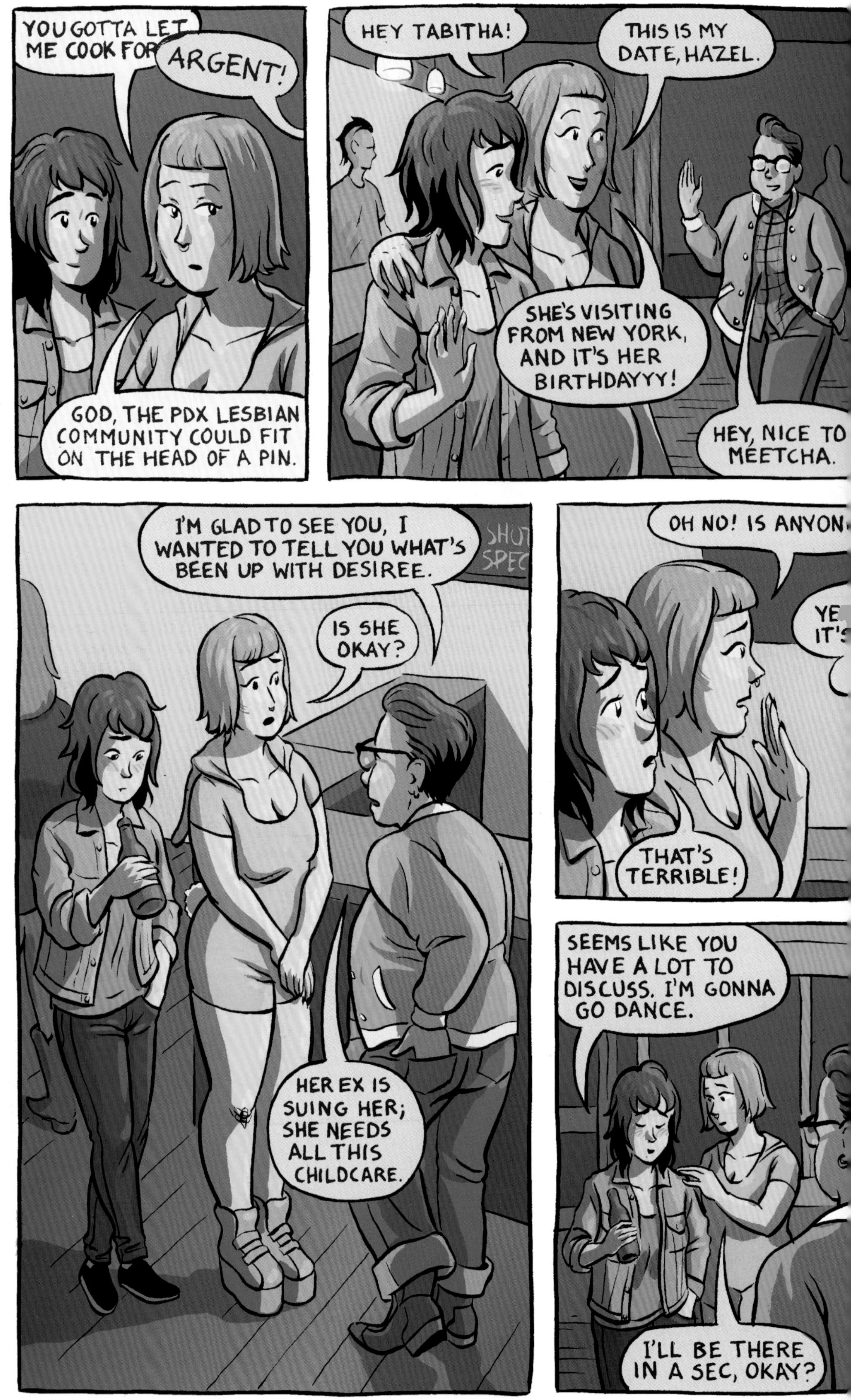
YOU GOTTA LET ME COOK FOR
ARGENT!
GOD, THE PDX LESBIAN COMMUNITY COULD FIT ON THE HEAD OF A PIN.
HEY TABITHA!
THIS IS MY DATE, HAZEL.
SHE'S VISITING FROM NEW YORK, AND IT'S HER BIRTHDAYYY!
HEY, NICE TO MEETCHA.
I'M GLAD TO SEE YOU, I WANTED TO TELL YOU WHAT'S BEEN UP WITH DESIREE.
IS SHE OKAY?
HER EX IS SUING HER; SHE NEEDS ALL THIS CHILDCARE.
OH NO! IS ANYON
THAT'S TERRIBLE!
SEEMS LIKE YOU HAVE A LOT TO DISCUSS. I'M GONNA GO DANCE.
I'LL BE THERE IN A SEC, OKAY?

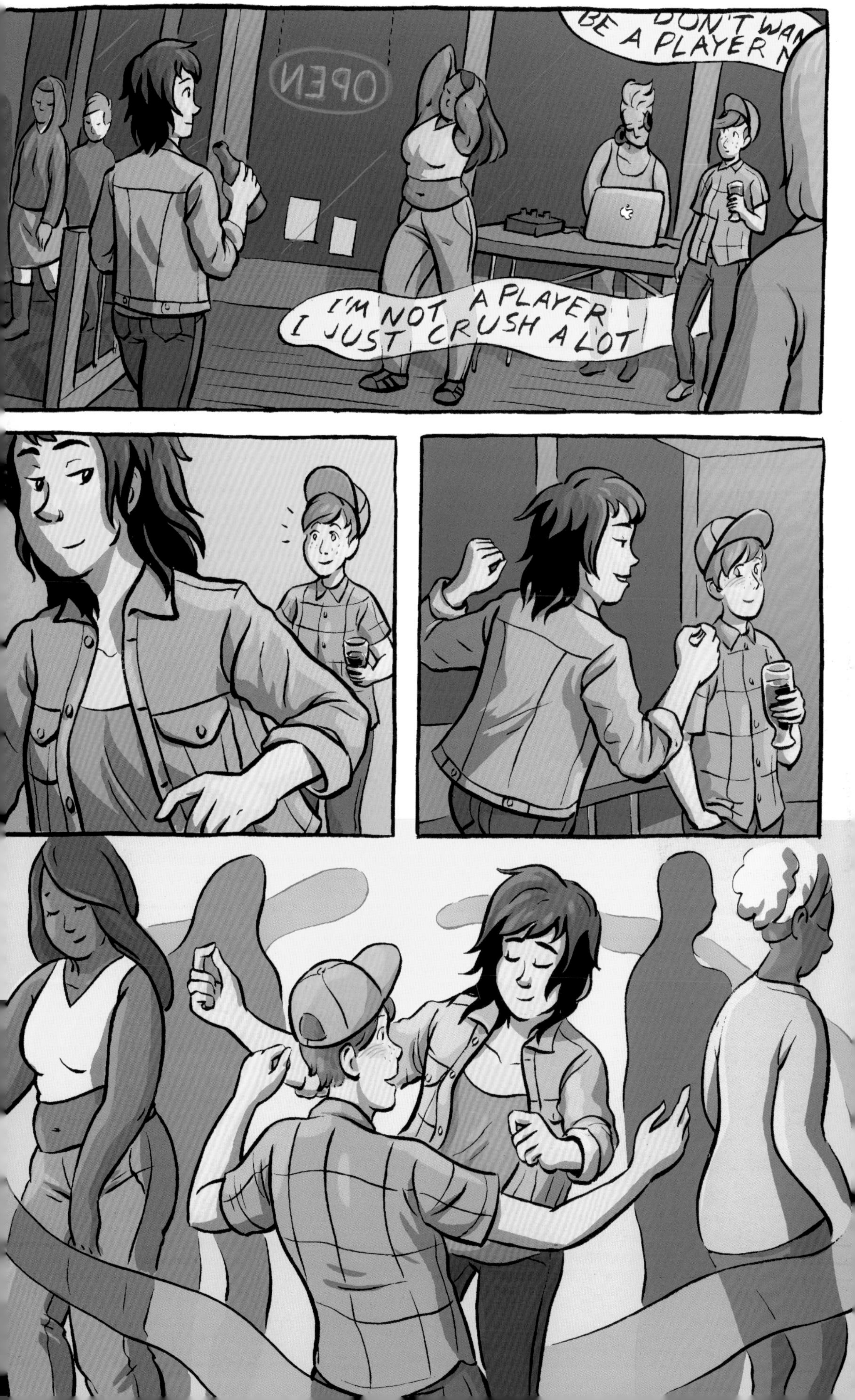

DON'T WAN
BE A PLAYER N
OPEN
I'M NOT A PLAYER
I JUST CRUSH A LOT

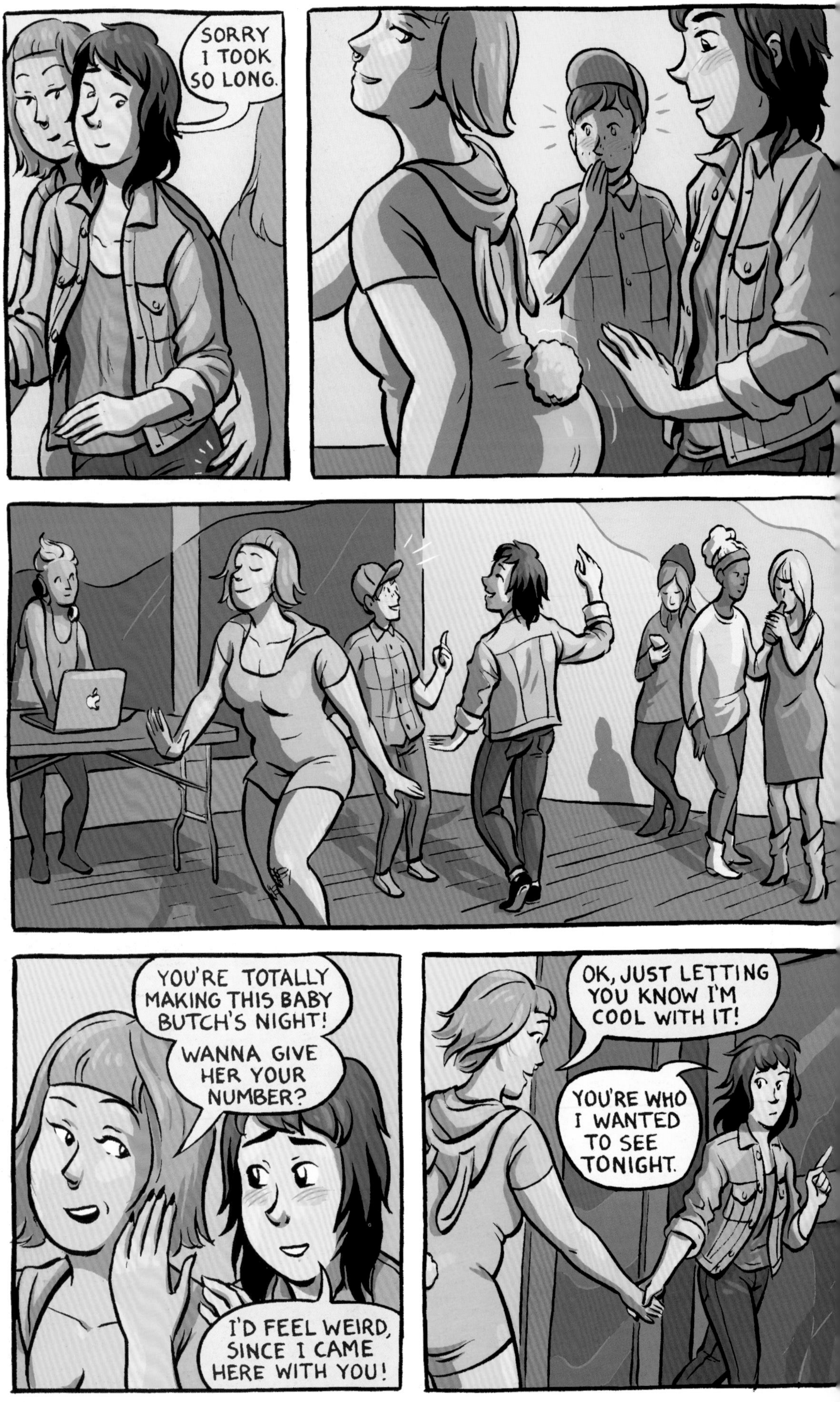
SORRY I TOOK SO LONG.
YOU'RE TOTALLY MAKING THIS BABY BUTCH'S NIGHT!
WANNA GIVE HER YOUR NUMBER?
I'D FEEL WEIRD, SINCE I CAME HERE WITH YOU!
OK, JUST LETTING YOU KNOW I'M COOL WITH IT!
YOU'RE WHO I WANTED TO SEE TONIGHT.

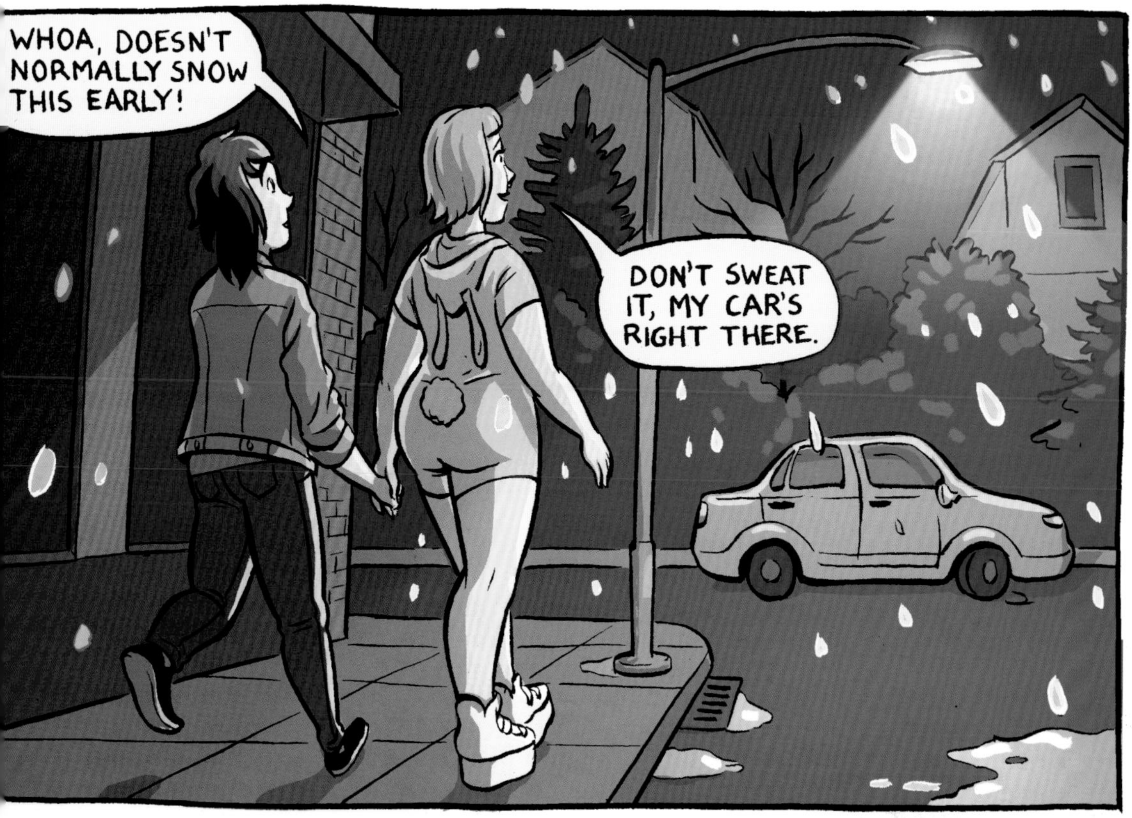
WHOA, DOESN'T NORMALLY SNOW THIS EARLY!
DON'T SWEAT IT, MY CAR'S RIGHT THERE.

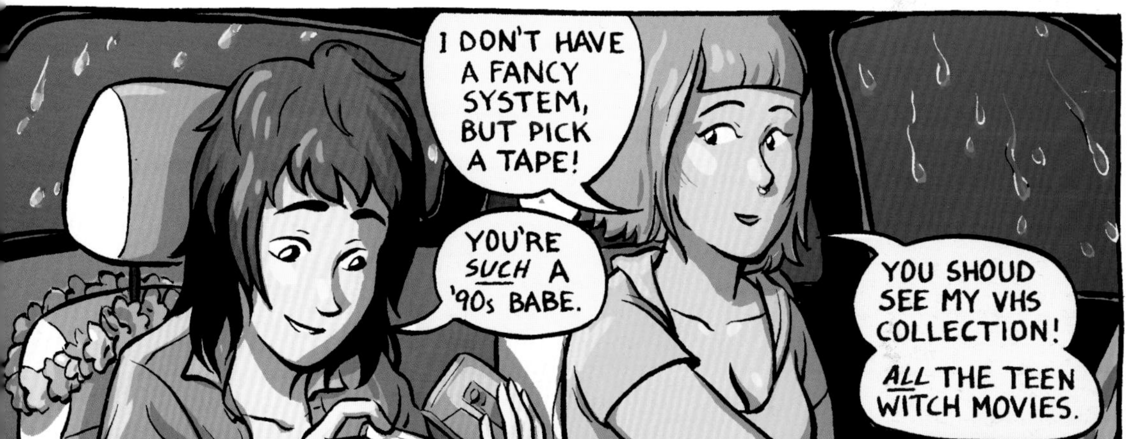
I DON'T HAVE A FANCY SYSTEM, BUT PICK A TAPE!
YOU'RE SUCH A '90s BABE.
YOU SHOUD SEE MY VHS COLLECTION!
ALL THE TEEN WITCH MOVIES.

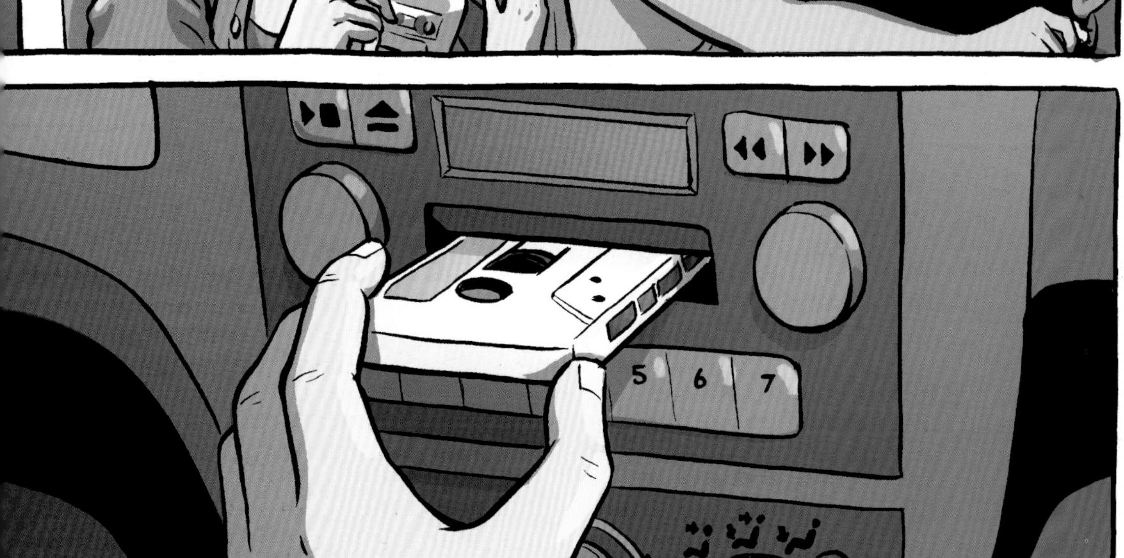
5 6 7

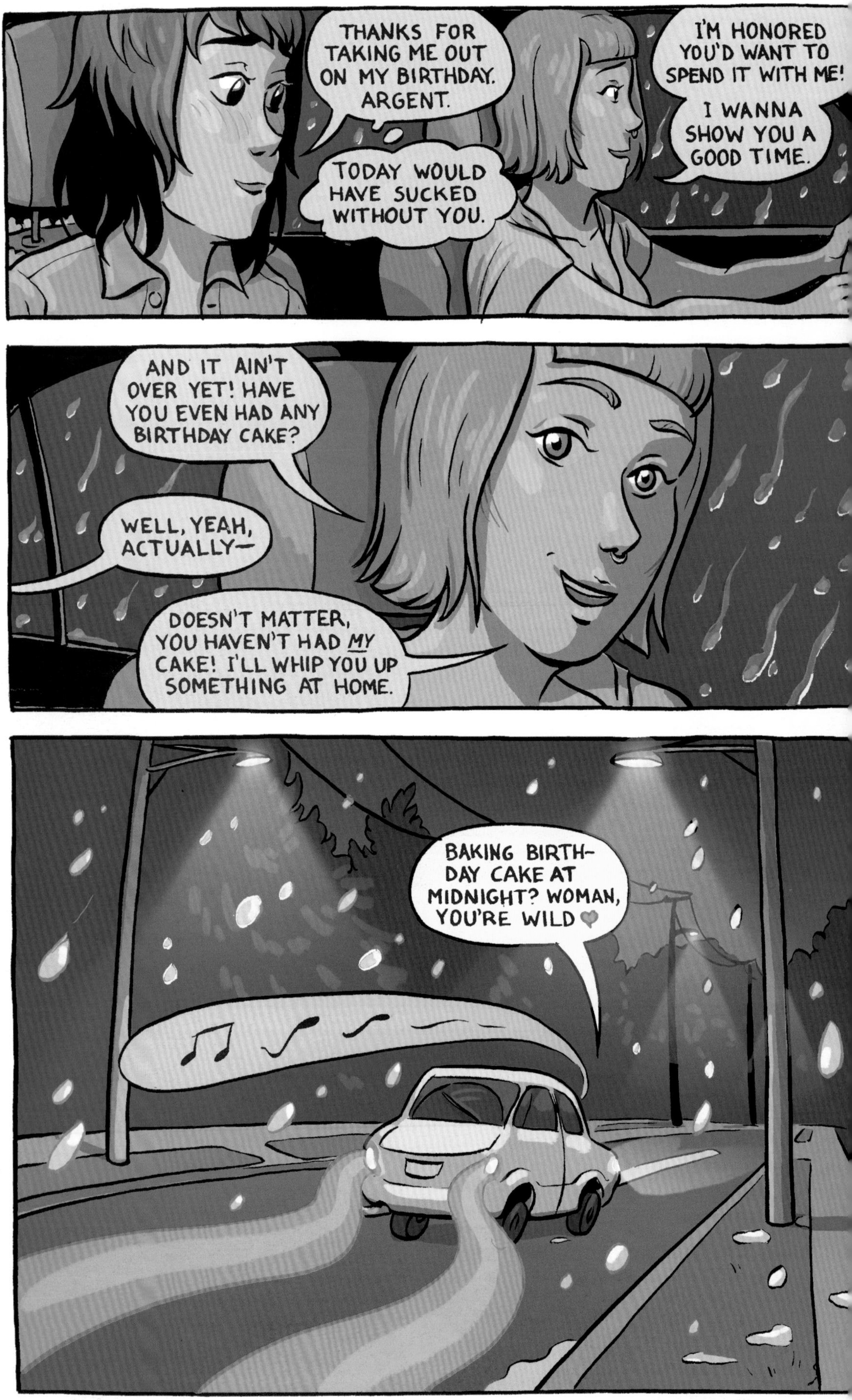
THANKS FOR TAKING ME OUT ON MY BIRTHDAY. ARGENT.
TODAY WOULD HAVE SUCKED WITHOUT YOU.
I'M HONORED YOU'D WANT TO SPEND IT WITH ME!
I WANNA SHOW YOU A GOOD TIME.
AND IT AIN'T OVER YET! HAVE YOU EVEN HAD ANY BIRTHDAY CAKE?
WELL, YEAH, ACTUALLY—
DOESN'T MATTER, YOU HAVEN'T HAD MY CAKE! I'LL WHIP YOU UP SOMETHING AT HOME.
BAKING BIRTHDAY CAKE AT MIDNIGHT? WOMAN, YOU'RE WILD

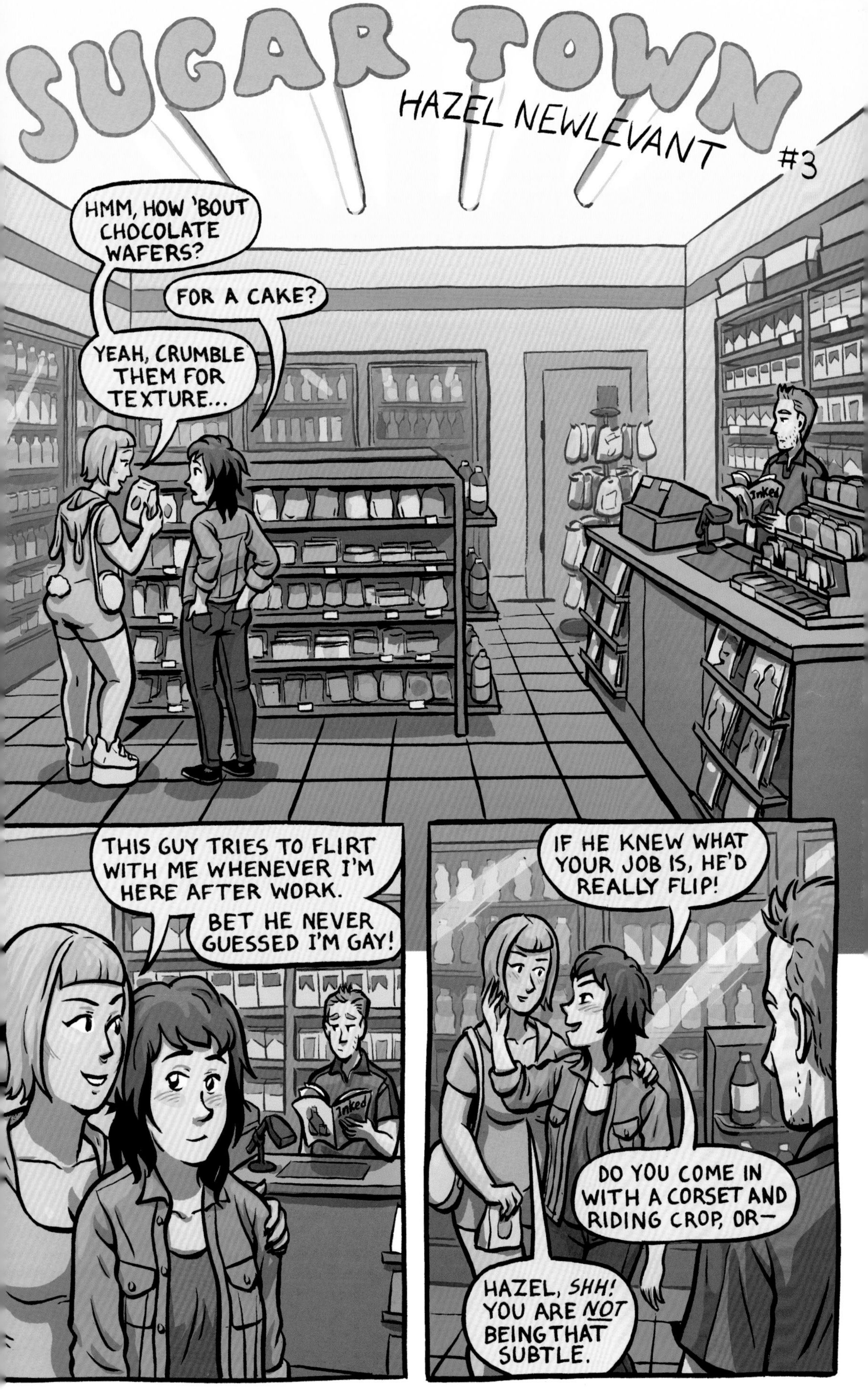
SUGAR TOWN
HAZEL NEWLEVANT
#3
HMM, HOW 'BOUT CHOCOLATE WAFERS?
FOR A CAKE?
YEAH, CRUMBLE THEM FOR TEXTURE...
Inked
THIS GUY TRIES TO FLIRT WITH ME WHENEVER I'M HERE AFTER WORK.
BET HE NEVER GUESSED I'M GAY!
Inked
IF HE KNEW WHAT YOUR JOB IS, HE'D REALLY FLIP!
DO YOU COME IN WITH A CORSET AND RIDING CROP, OR—
HAZEL, SHH! YOU ARE NOT BEING THAT SUBTLE.

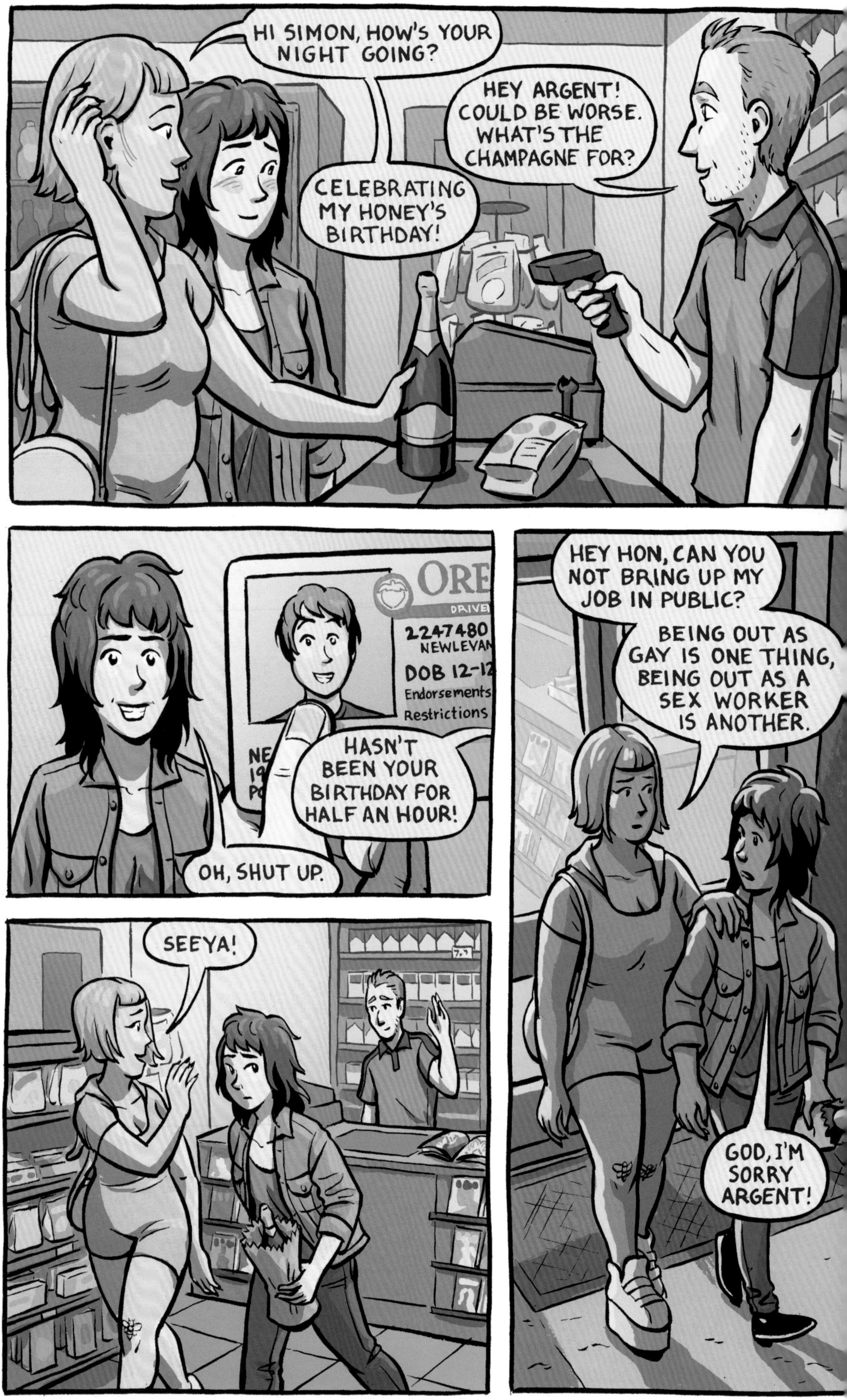
HI SIMON, HOW'S YOUR NIGHT GOING?
HEY ARGENT! COULD BE WORSE. WHAT'S THE CHAMPAGNE FOR?
CELEBRATING MY HONEY'S BIRTHDAY!
ORE
DRIVE
2247480
NEWLEVAN
DOB 12-12
Endorsements
Restrictions
HASN'T BEEN YOUR BIRTHDAY FOR HALF AN HOUR!
OH, SHUT UP.
HEY HON, CAN YOU NOT BRING UP MY JOB IN PUBLIC?
BEING OUT AS GAY IS ONE THING, BEING OUT AS A SEX WORKER IS ANOTHER.
SEEYA!
GOD, I'M SORRY ARGENT!

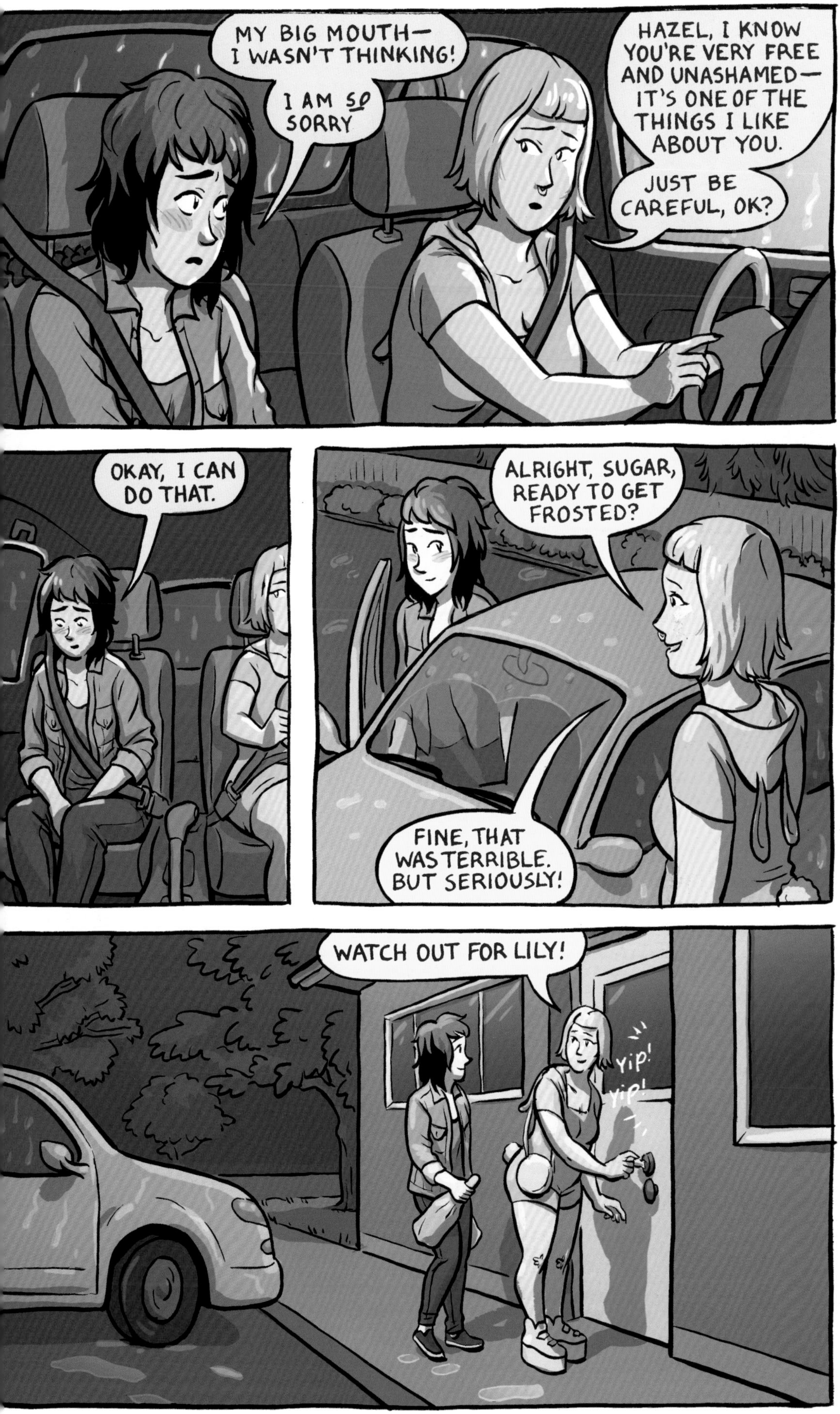
MY BIG MOUTH— I WASN'T THINKING!
I AM SO SORRY
HAZEL, I KNOW YOU'RE VERY FREE AND UNASHAMED— IT'S ONE OF THE THINGS I LIKE ABOUT YOU.
JUST BE CAREFUL, OK?
OKAY, I CAN DO THAT.
ALRIGHT, SUGAR, READY TO GET FROSTED?
FINE, THAT WAS TERRIBLE. BUT SERIOUSLY!
WATCH OUT FOR LILY!
YIP!
YIP!

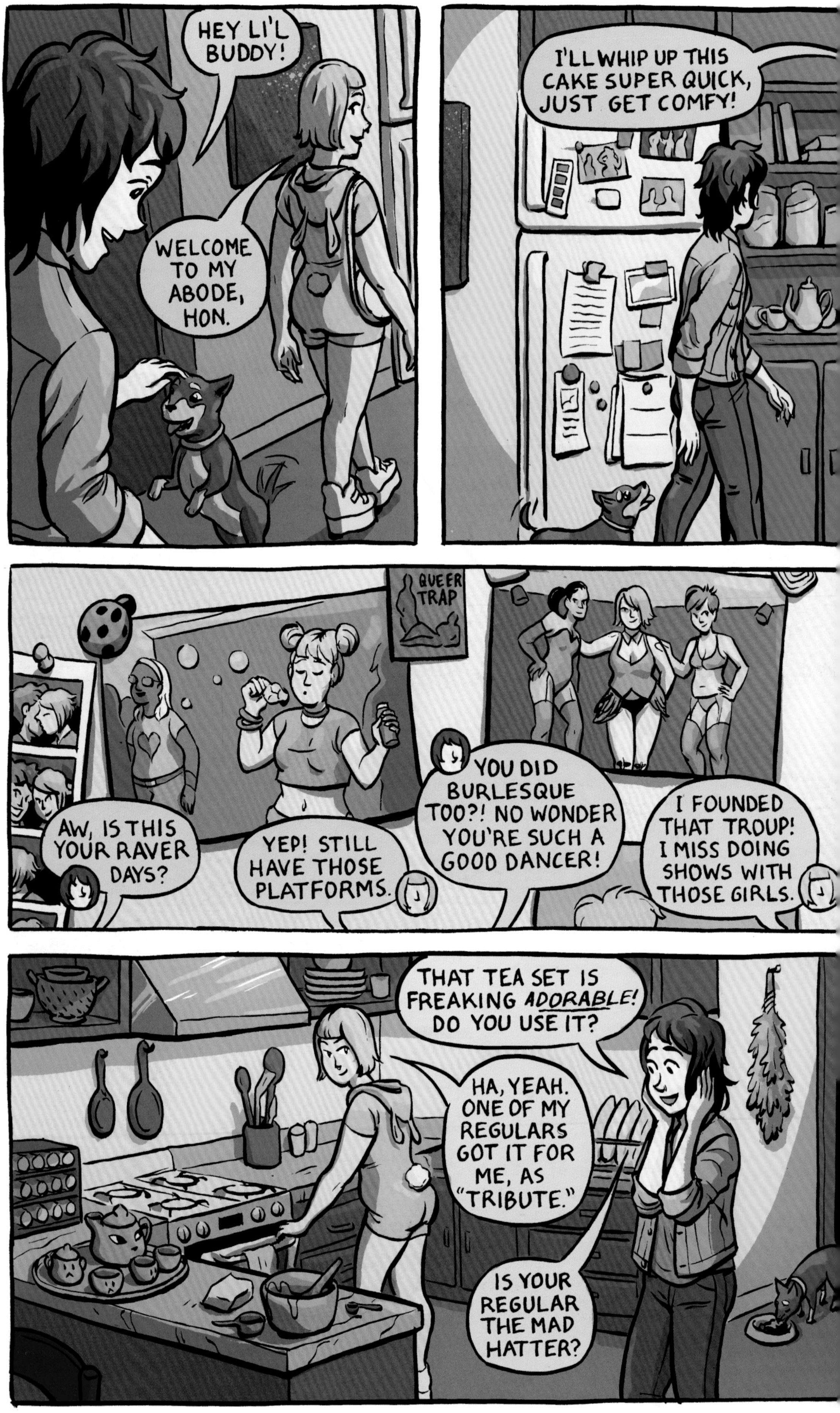
HEY LI'L BUDDY!
WELCOME TO MY ABODE, HON.
I'LL WHIP UP THIS CAKE SUPER QUICK, JUST GET COMFY!
QUEER TRAP
AW, IS THIS YOUR RAVER DAYS?
YEP! STILL HAVE THOSE PLATFORMS.
YOU DID BURLESQUE TOO?! NO WONDER YOU'RE SUCH A GOOD DANCER!
I FOUNDED THAT TROUP! I MISS DOING SHOWS WITH THOSE GIRLS.
THAT TEA SET IS FREAKING *ADORABLE*! DO YOU USE IT?
HA, YEAH. ONE OF MY REGULARS GOT IT FOR ME, AS "TRIBUTE."
IS YOUR REGULAR THE MAD HATTER?

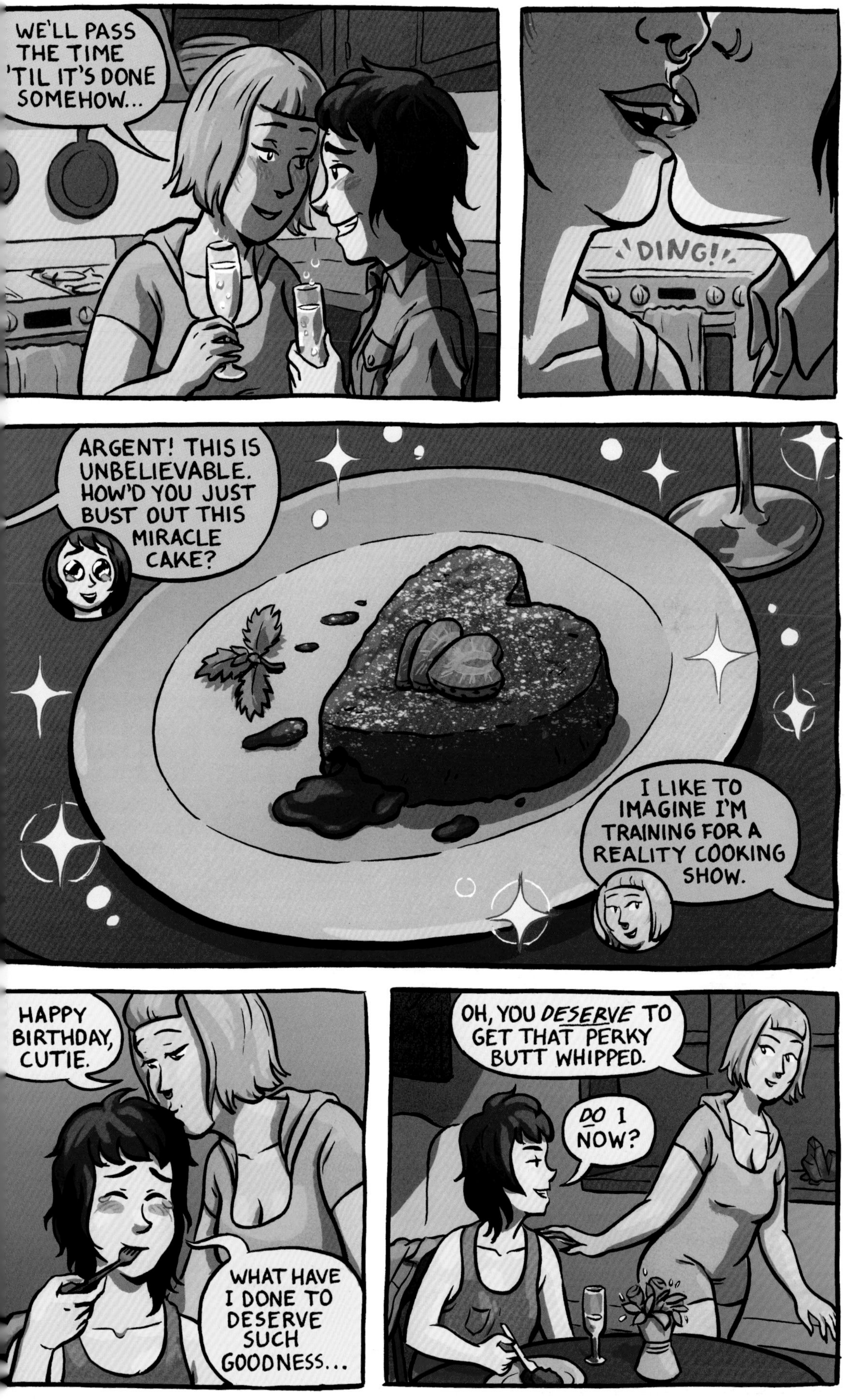
WE'LL PASS THE TIME 'TIL IT'S DONE SOMEHOW...
DING!!
ARGENT! THIS IS UNBELIEVABLE. HOW'D YOU JUST BUST OUT THIS MIRACLE CAKE?
I LIKE TO IMAGINE I'M TRAINING FOR A REALITY COOKING SHOW.
HAPPY BIRTHDAY, CUTIE.
WHAT HAVE I DONE TO DESERVE SUCH GOODNESS...
OH, YOU DESERVE TO GET THAT PERKY BUTT WHIPPED.
DO I NOW?

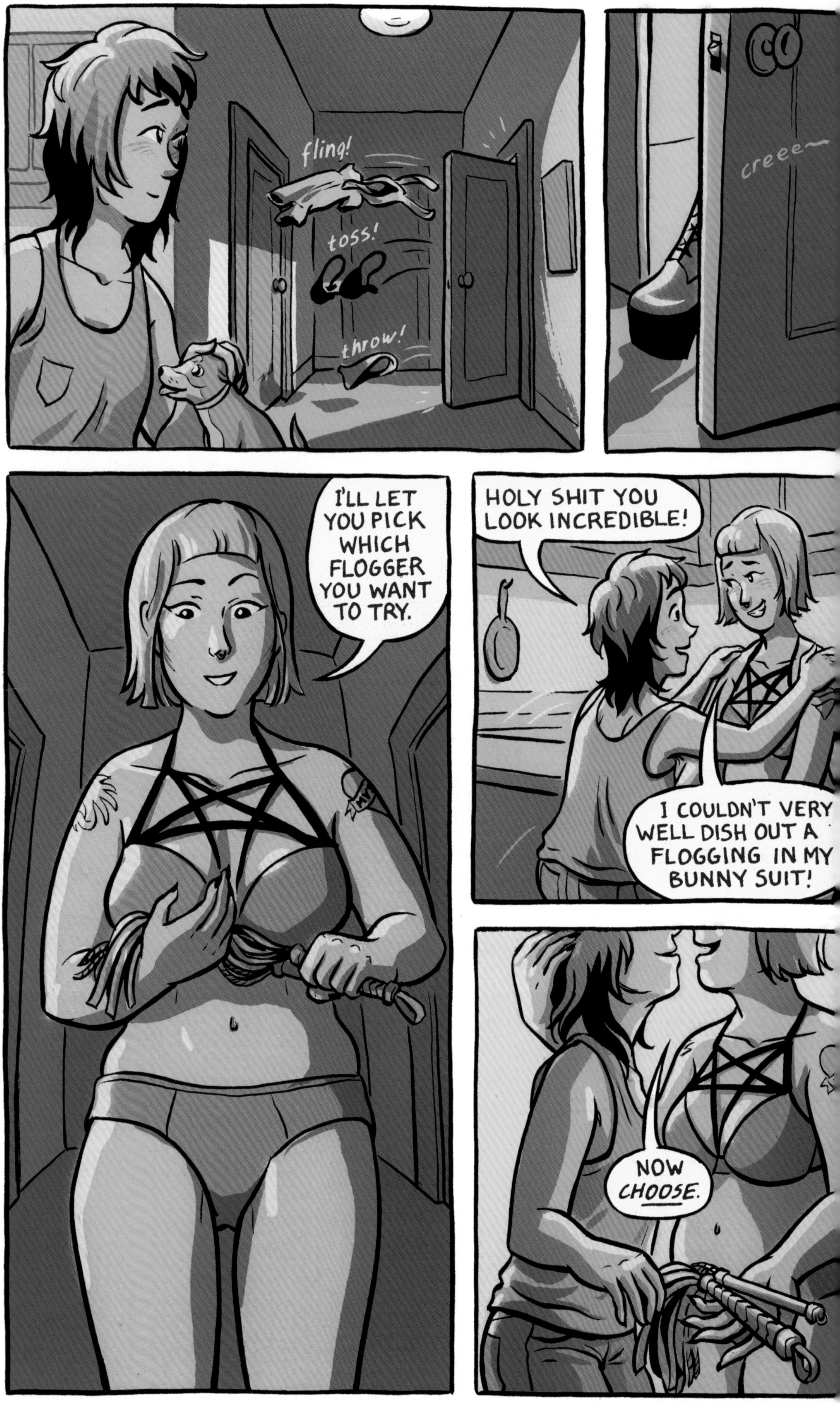
fling!
toss!
throw!
creee~
I'LL LET YOU PICK WHICH FLOGGER YOU WANT TO TRY.
HOLY SHIT YOU LOOK INCREDIBLE!
I COULDN'T VERY WELL DISH OUT A FLOGGING IN MY BUNNY SUIT!
NOW CHOOSE.

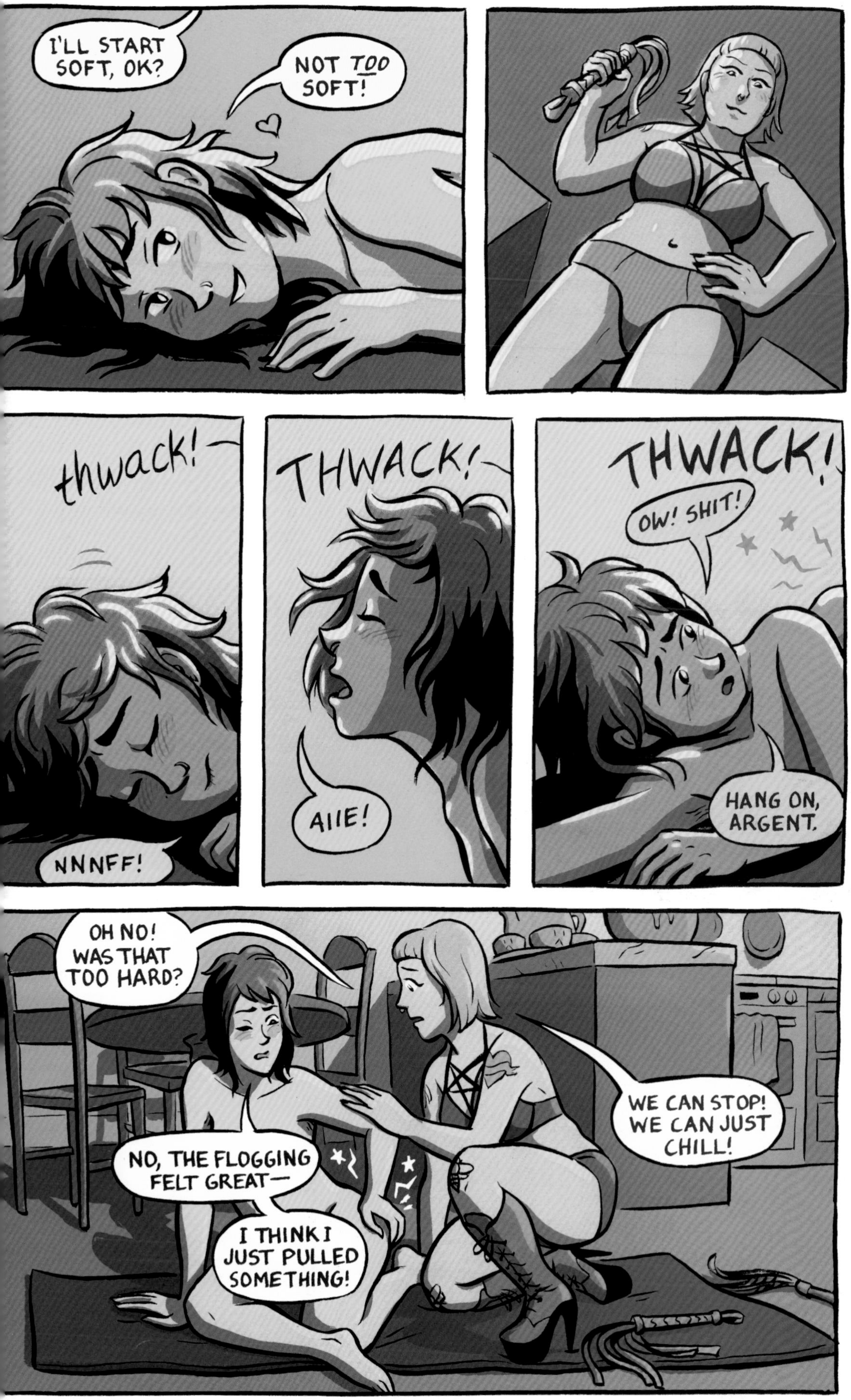
I'LL START SOFT, OK?
NOT TOO SOFT!
thwack!
NNNFF!
THWACK!
AIIE!
THWACK!
OW! SHIT!
HANG ON, ARGENT.
OH NO! WAS THAT TOO HARD?
WE CAN STOP! WE CAN JUST CHILL!
NO, THE FLOGGING FELT GREAT—
I THINK I JUST PULLED SOMETHING!

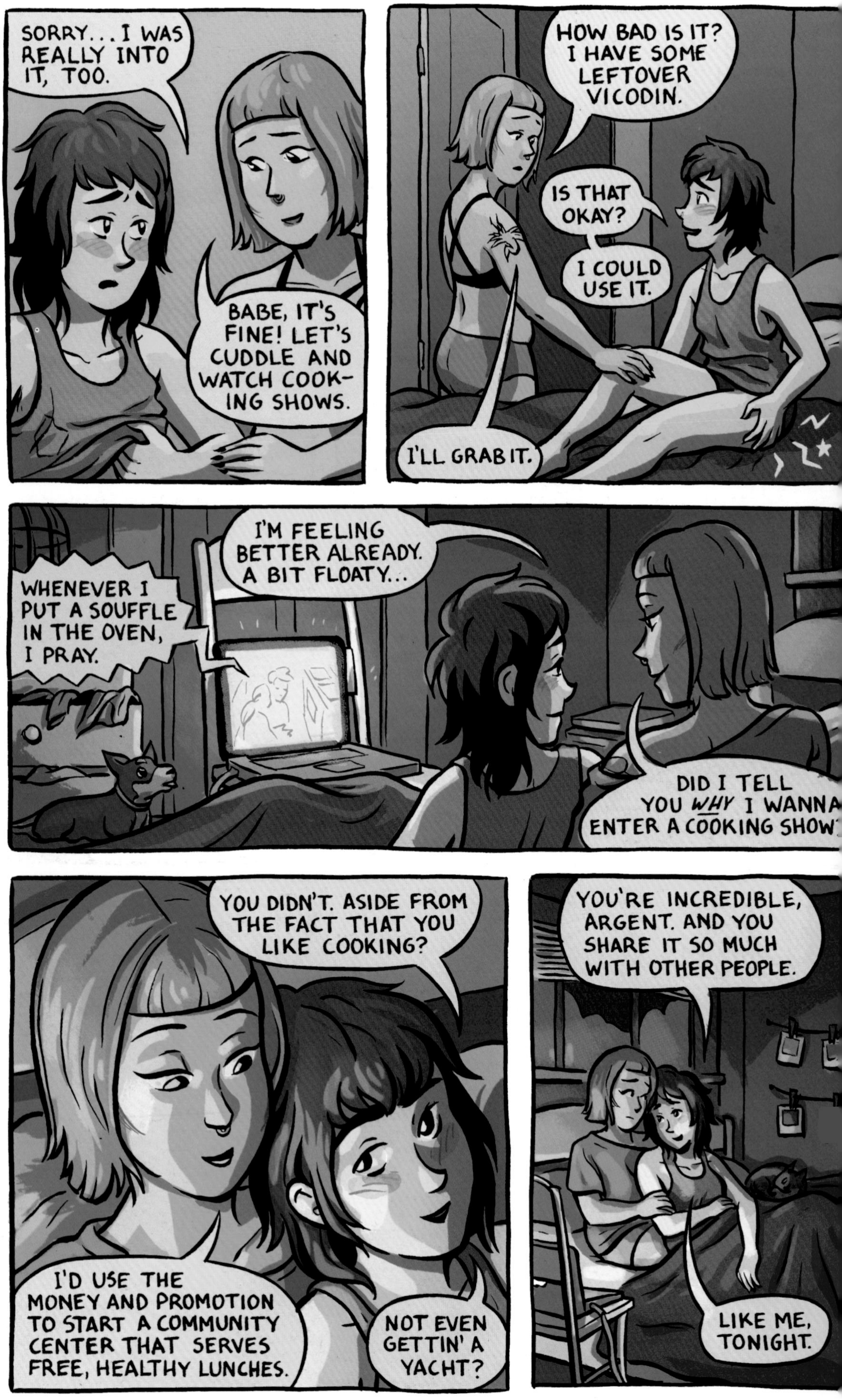
SORRY... I WAS REALLY INTO IT, TOO.
BABE, IT'S FINE! LET'S CUDDLE AND WATCH COOK-ING SHOWS.
HOW BAD IS IT? I HAVE SOME LEFTOVER VICODIN.
IS THAT OKAY?
I COULD USE IT.
I'LL GRAB IT.
WHENEVER I PUT A SOUFFLE IN THE OVEN, I PRAY.
I'M FEELING BETTER ALREADY. A BIT FLOATY...
DID I TELL YOU WHY I WANNA ENTER A COOKING SHOW?
YOU DIDN'T. ASIDE FROM THE FACT THAT YOU LIKE COOKING?
I'D USE THE MONEY AND PROMOTION TO START A COMMUNITY CENTER THAT SERVES FREE, HEALTHY LUNCHES.
NOT EVEN GETTIN' A YACHT?
YOU'RE INCREDIBLE, ARGENT. AND YOU SHARE IT SO MUCH WITH OTHER PEOPLE.
LIKE ME, TONIGHT.

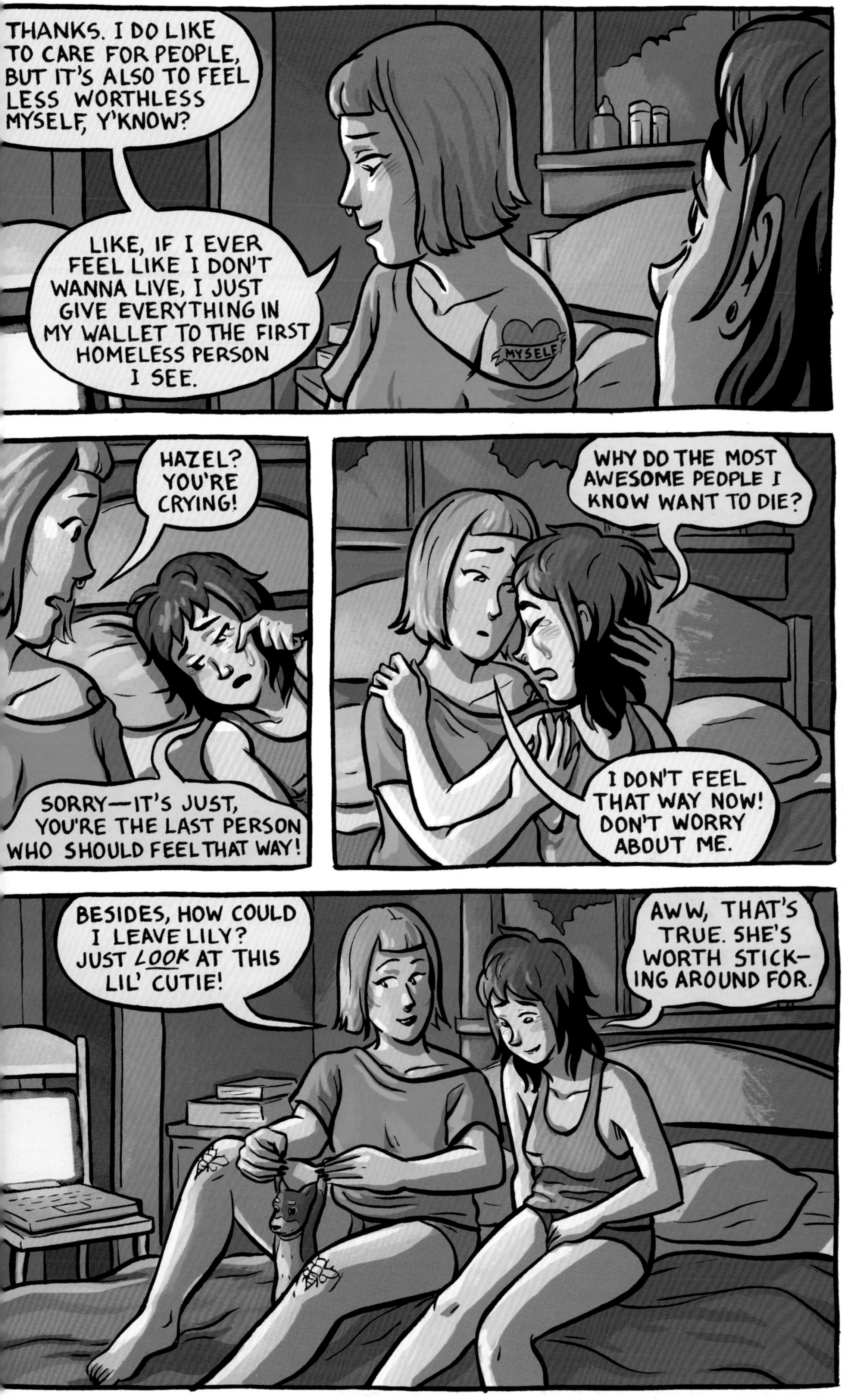
THANKS. I DO LIKE TO CARE FOR PEOPLE, BUT IT'S ALSO TO FEEL LESS WORTHLESS MYSELF, Y'KNOW?
LIKE, IF I EVER FEEL LIKE I DON'T WANNA LIVE, I JUST GIVE EVERYTHING IN MY WALLET TO THE FIRST HOMELESS PERSON I SEE.
MYSELF
HAZEL? YOU'RE CRYING!
SORRY—IT'S JUST, YOU'RE THE LAST PERSON WHO SHOULD FEEL THAT WAY!
WHY DO THE MOST AWESOME PEOPLE I KNOW WANT TO DIE?
I DON'T FEEL THAT WAY NOW! DON'T WORRY ABOUT ME.
BESIDES, HOW COULD I LEAVE LILY? JUST LOOK AT THIS LIL' CUTIE!
AWW, THAT'S TRUE. SHE'S WORTH STICK-ING AROUND FOR.

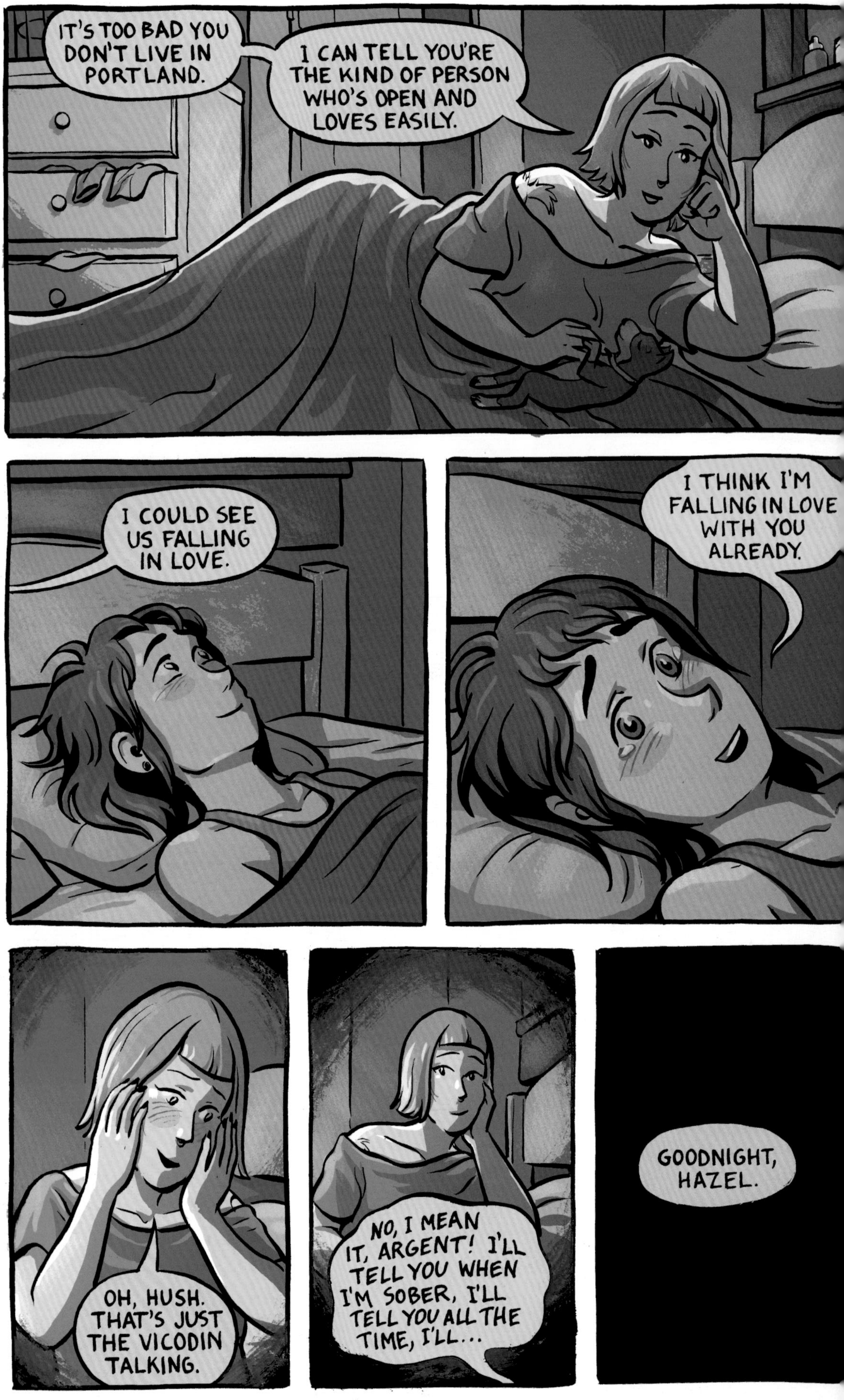
IT'S TOO BAD YOU DON'T LIVE IN PORTLAND.
I CAN TELL YOU'RE THE KIND OF PERSON WHO'S OPEN AND LOVES EASILY.
I COULD SEE US FALLING IN LOVE.
I THINK I'M FALLING IN LOVE WITH YOU ALREADY.
OH, HUSH. THAT'S JUST THE VICODIN TALKING.
NO, I MEAN IT, ARGENT! I'LL TELL YOU WHEN I'M SOBER, I'LL TELL YOU ALL THE TIME, I'LL...
GOODNIGHT, HAZEL.

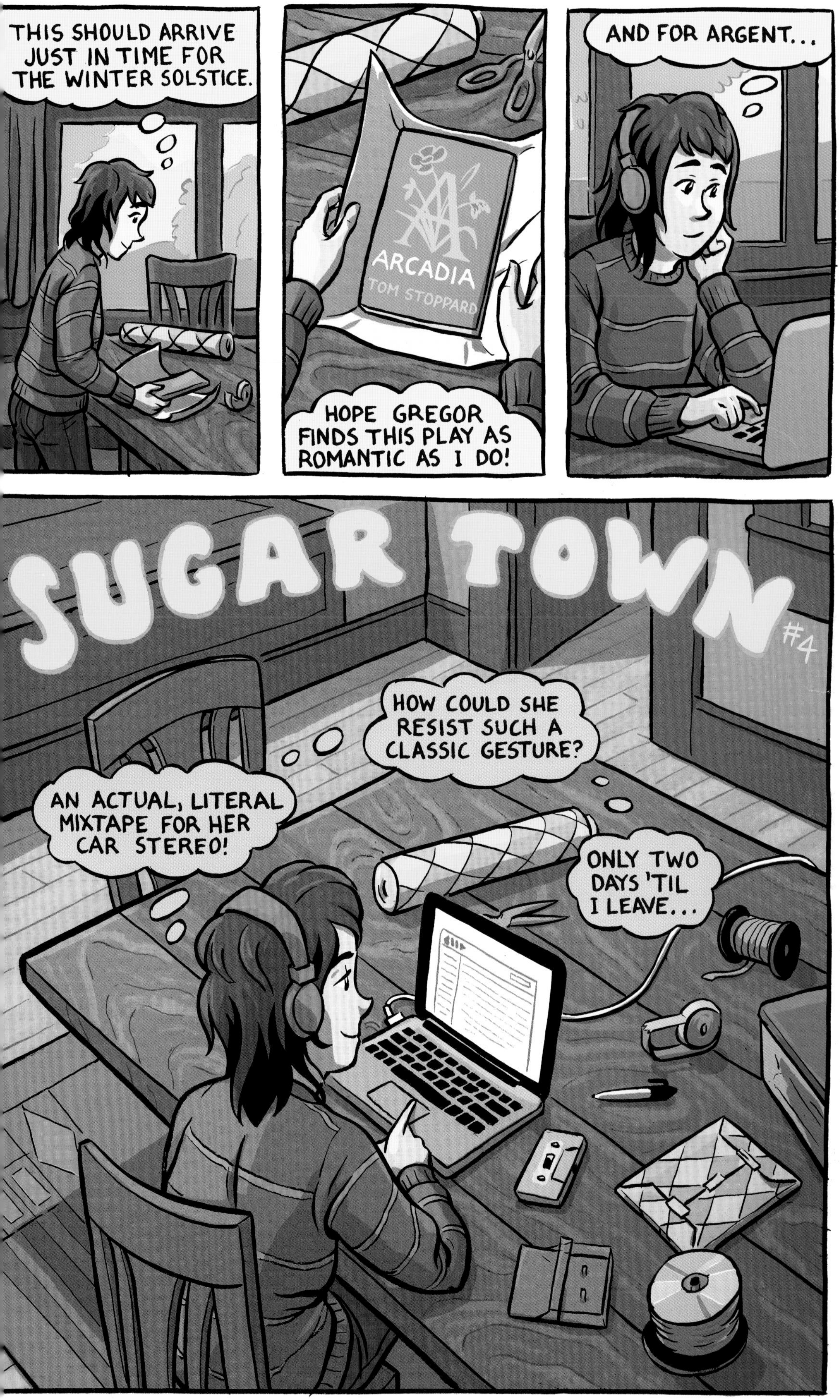
THIS SHOULD ARRIVE JUST IN TIME FOR THE WINTER SOLSTICE.
ARCADIA
TOM STOPPARD
HOPE GREGOR FINDS THIS PLAY AS ROMANTIC AS I DO!
AND FOR ARGENT...
SUGAR TOWN #4
HOW COULD SHE RESIST SUCH A CLASSIC GESTURE?
AN ACTUAL, LITERAL MIXTAPE FOR HER CAR STEREO!
ONLY TWO DAYS 'TIL I LEAVE...

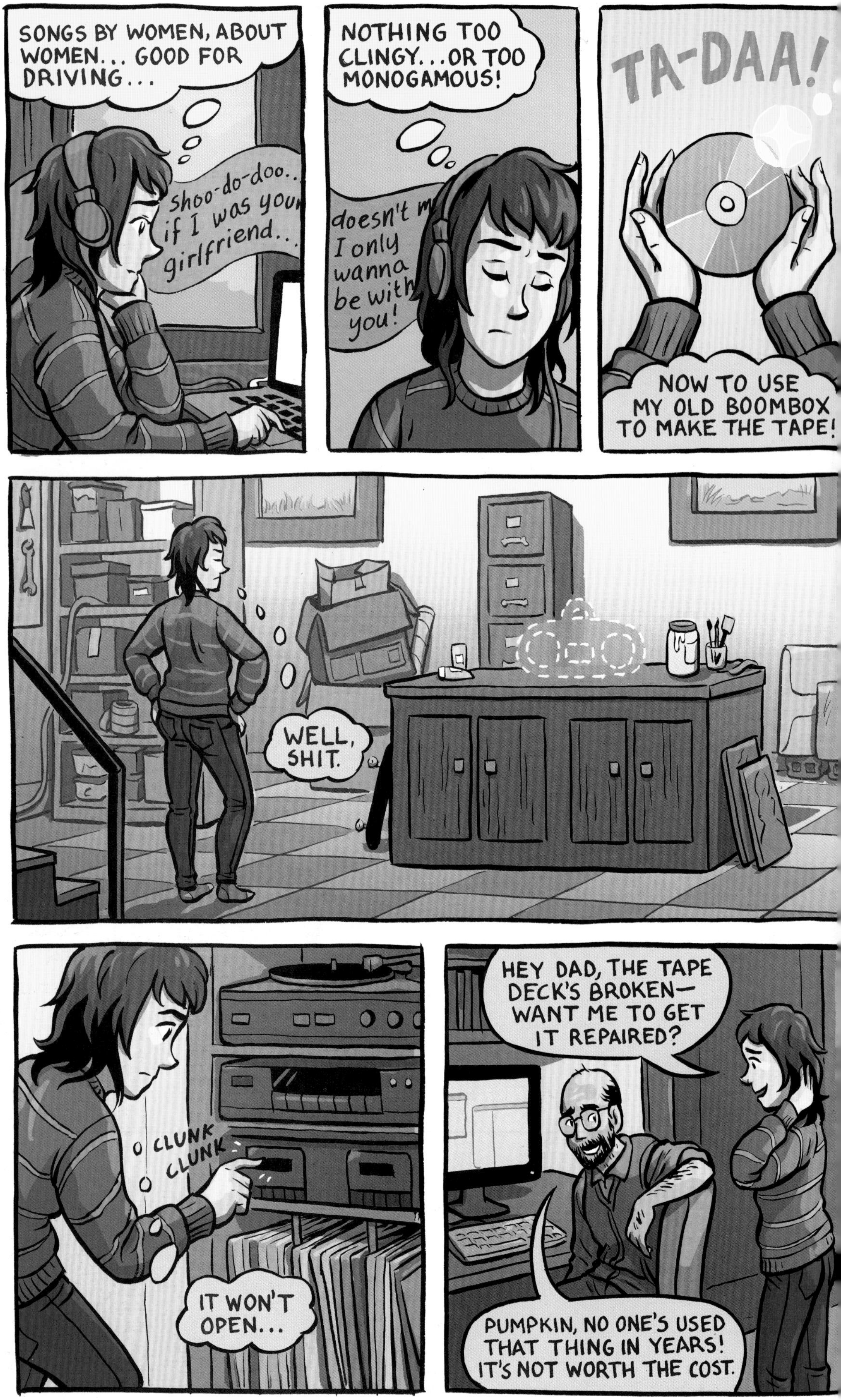
SONGS BY WOMEN, ABOUT WOMEN... GOOD FOR DRIVING...
Shoo-do-doo... if I was your girlfriend...
NOTHING TOO CLINGY...OR TOO MONOGAMOUS!
doesn't m I only wanna be with you!
TA-DAA!
NOW TO USE MY OLD BOOMBOX TO MAKE THE TAPE!
WELL, SHIT.
CLUNK CLUNK
IT WON'T OPEN...
HEY DAD, THE TAPE DECK'S BROKEN— WANT ME TO GET IT REPAIRED?
PUMPKIN, NO ONE'S USED THAT THING IN YEARS! IT'S NOT WORTH THE COST.

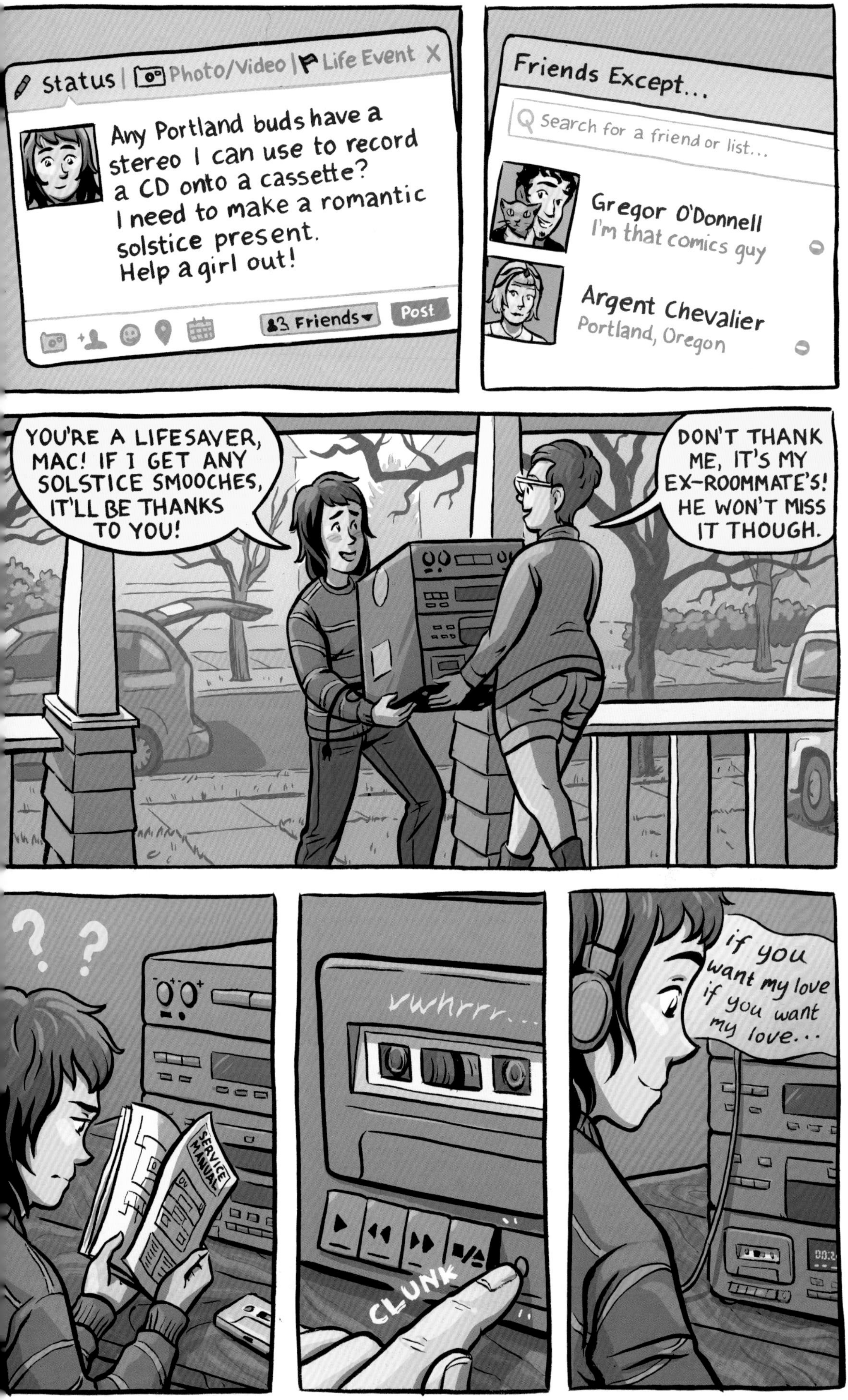
Status | Photo/Video | Life Event X
Any Portland buds have a stereo I can use to record a CD onto a cassette? I need to make a romantic solstice present. Help a girl out!
Friends
Post
Friends Except...
Search for a friend or list...
Gregor O'Donnell
I'm that comics guy
Argent Chevalier
Portland, Oregon
YOU'RE A LIFESAVER, MAC! IF I GET ANY SOLSTICE SMOOCHES, IT'LL BE THANKS TO YOU!
DON'T THANK ME, IT'S MY EX-ROOMMATE'S! HE WON'T MISS IT THOUGH.
? ?
SERVICE MANUAL
vwhrrr...
CLUNK
if you want my love if you want my love...

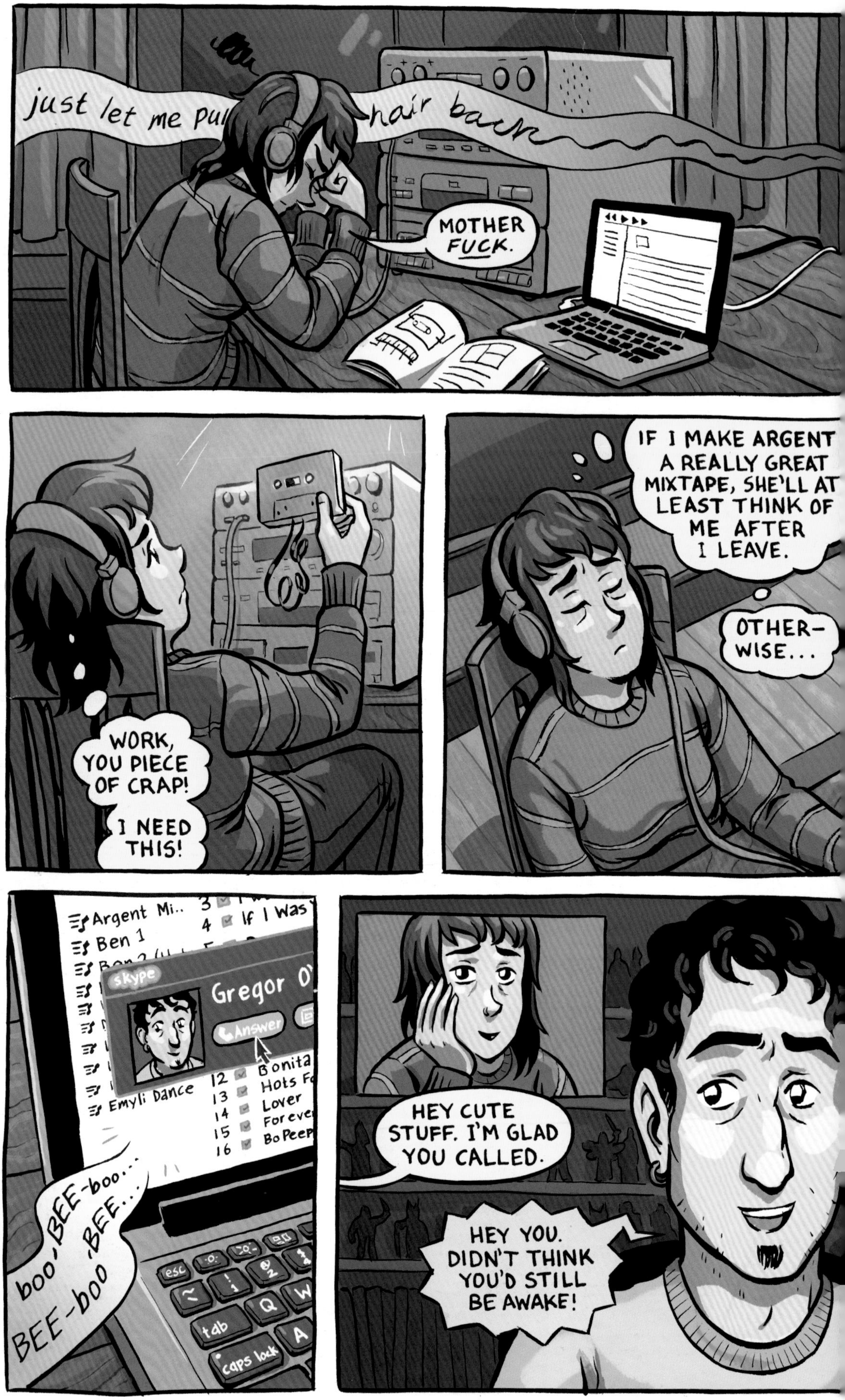
just let me pu
hair back
MOTHER FUCK.
WORK, YOU PIECE OF CRAP!
I NEED THIS!
IF I MAKE ARGENT A REALLY GREAT MIXTAPE, SHE'LL AT LEAST THINK OF ME AFTER I LEAVE.
OTHER- WISE...
Argent Mi..
Ben 1
If I Was
skype
Gregor O'
Answer
Emyli Dance
12 Bonita
Hots F
13 Lover
14 Forever
15 Bo Peep
16
boo, BEE-boo...
BEE-boo BEE...
esc
tab
caps lock
HEY CUTE STUFF. I'M GLAD YOU CALLED.
HEY YOU. DIDN'T THINK YOU'D STILL BE AWAKE!

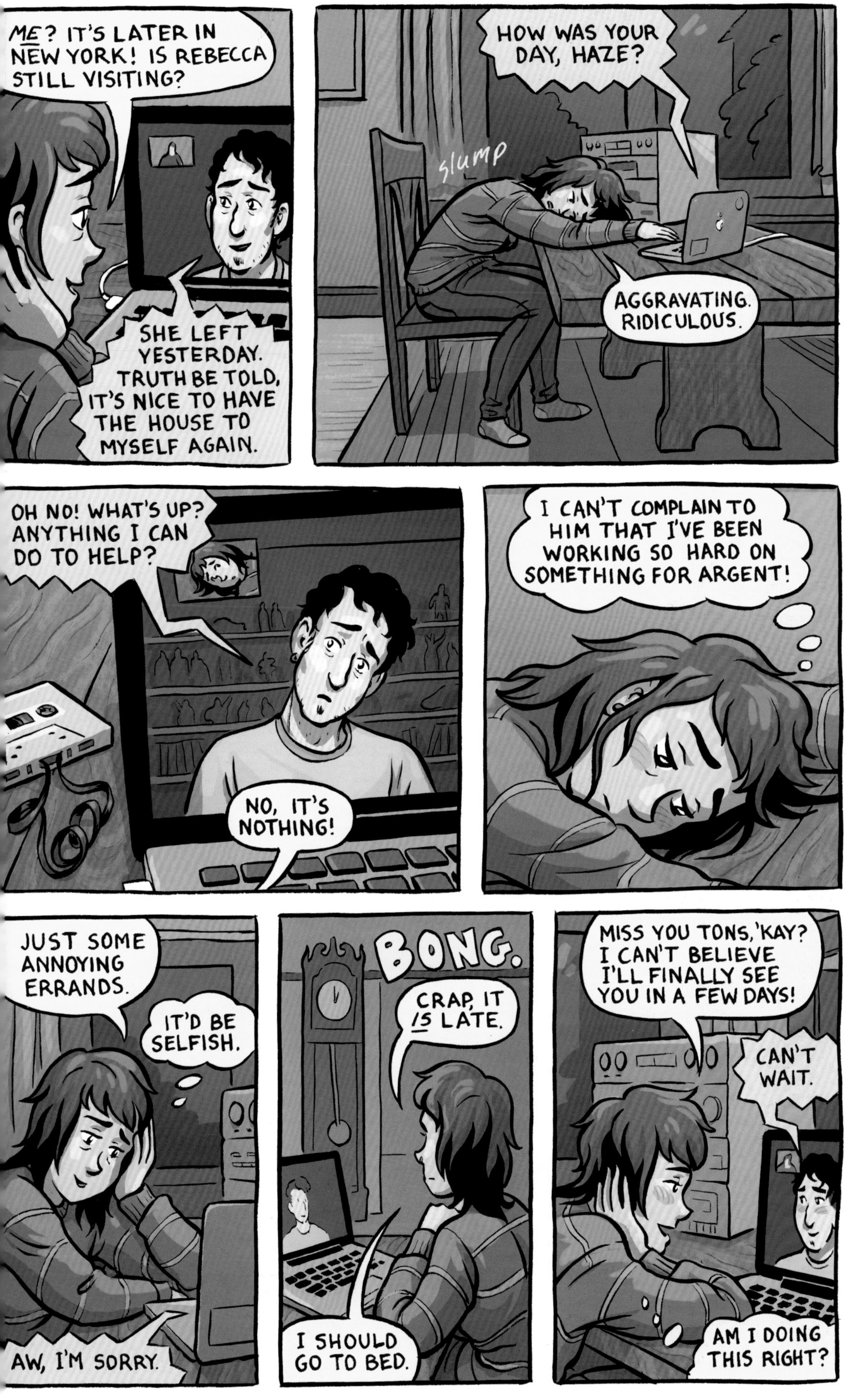

ME? IT'S LATER IN NEW YORK! IS REBECCA STILL VISITING?
SHE LEFT YESTERDAY. TRUTH BE TOLD, IT'S NICE TO HAVE THE HOUSE TO MYSELF AGAIN.
HOW WAS YOUR DAY, HAZE?
slump
AGGRAVATING. RIDICULOUS.
OH NO! WHAT'S UP? ANYTHING I CAN DO TO HELP?
NO, IT'S NOTHING!
I CAN'T COMPLAIN TO HIM THAT I'VE BEEN WORKING SO HARD ON SOMETHING FOR ARGENT!
JUST SOME ANNOYING ERRANDS.
IT'D BE SELFISH.
AW, I'M SORRY.
BONG.
CRAP, IT IS LATE.
I SHOULD GO TO BED.
MISS YOU TONS, 'KAY? I CAN'T BELIEVE I'LL FINALLY SEE YOU IN A FEW DAYS!
CAN'T WAIT.
AM I DOING THIS RIGHT?

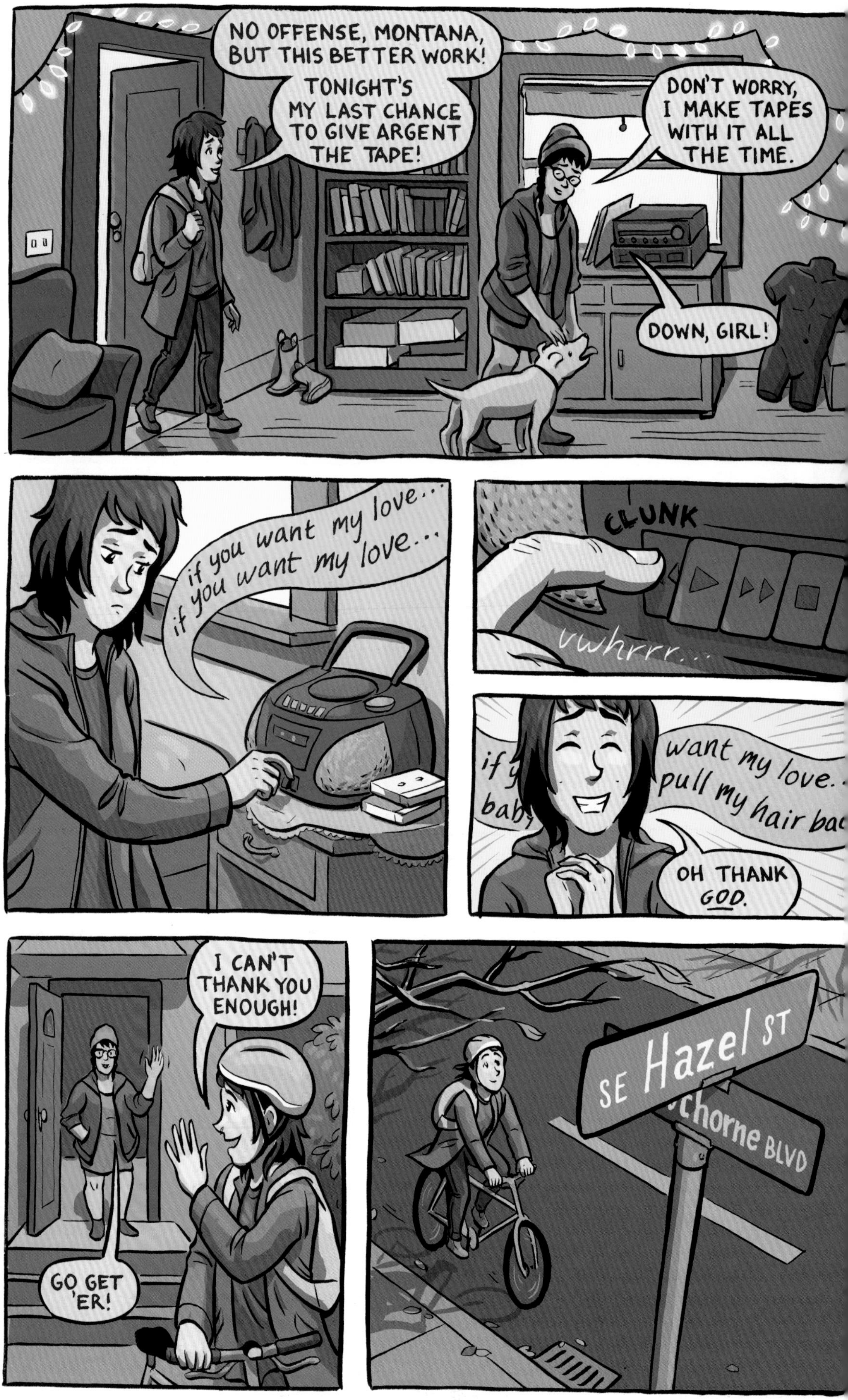
NO OFFENSE, MONTANA, BUT THIS BETTER WORK!
TONIGHT'S MY LAST CHANCE TO GIVE ARGENT THE TAPE!
DON'T WORRY, I MAKE TAPES WITH IT ALL THE TIME.
DOWN, GIRL!
if you want my love... if you want my love...
CLUNK
vwhrrr...
want my love... pull my hair ba
OH THANK GOD.
I CAN'T THANK YOU ENOUGH!
GO GET 'ER!
SE Hazel ST
thorne BLVD

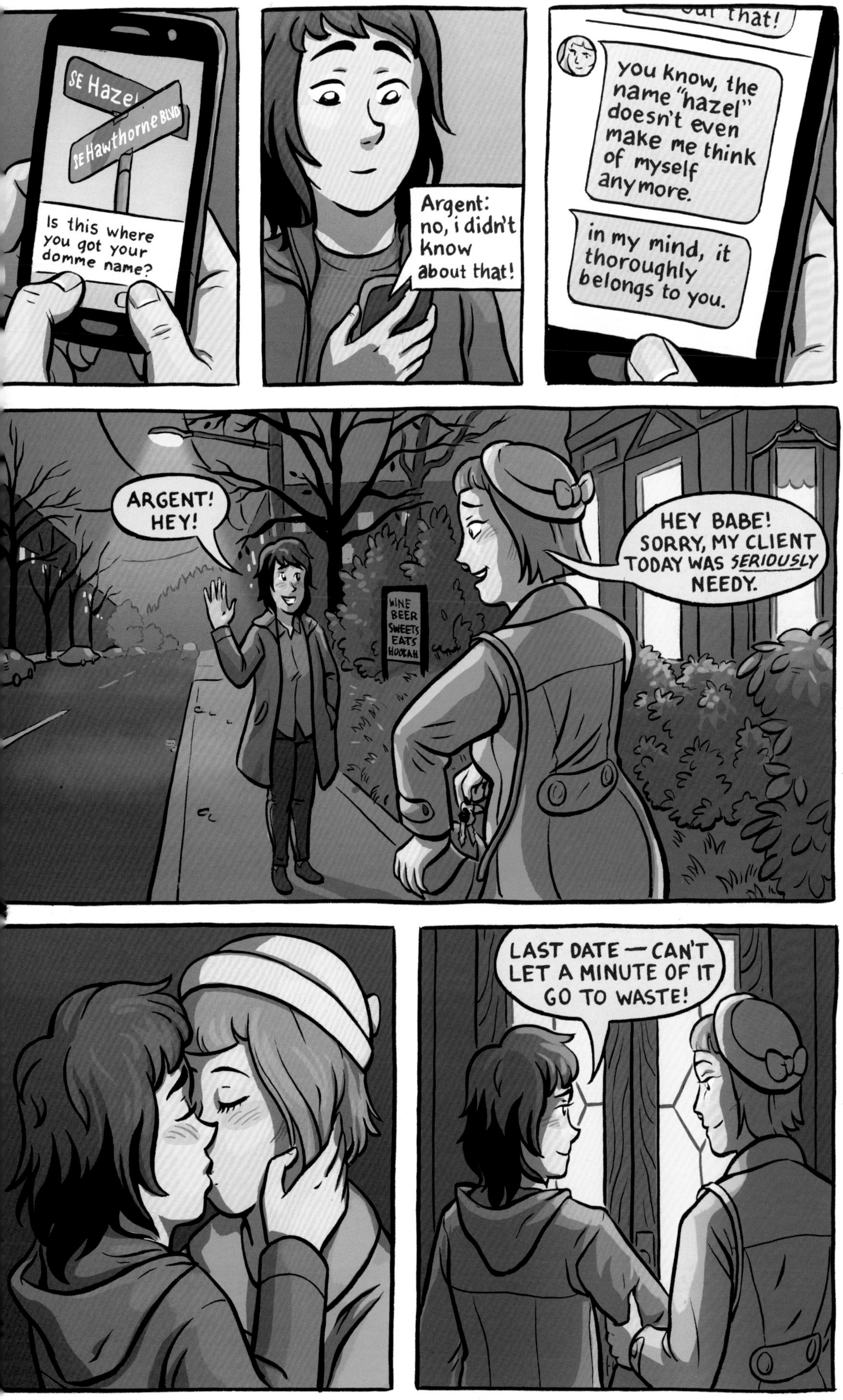
SE Hazel
SE Hawthorne BLVD
Is this where you got your domme name?
Argent: no, i didn't know about that!
...out that!
you know, the name "hazel" doesn't even make me think of myself anymore.
in my mind, it thoroughly belongs to you.
ARGENT! HEY!
WINE BEER SWEETS EATS HOOKAH
HEY BABE! SORRY, MY CLIENT TODAY WAS SERIOUSLY NEEDY.
LAST DATE — CAN'T LET A MINUTE OF IT GO TO WASTE!

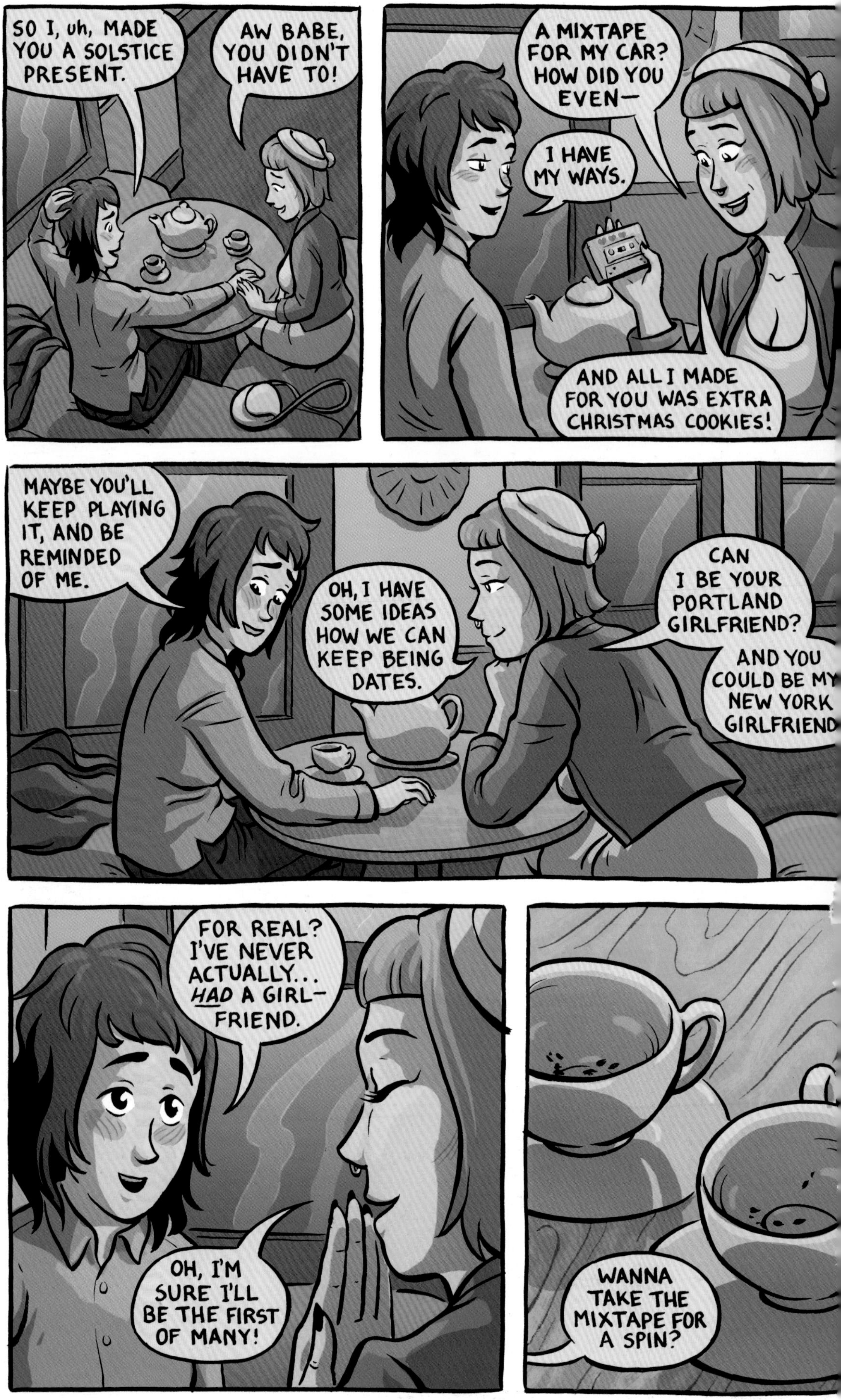
SO I, uh, MADE YOU A SOLSTICE PRESENT.
AW BABE, YOU DIDN'T HAVE TO!
A MIXTAPE FOR MY CAR? HOW DID YOU EVEN—
I HAVE MY WAYS.
AND ALL I MADE FOR YOU WAS EXTRA CHRISTMAS COOKIES!
MAYBE YOU'LL KEEP PLAYING IT, AND BE REMINDED OF ME.
OH, I HAVE SOME IDEAS HOW WE CAN KEEP BEING DATES.
CAN I BE YOUR PORTLAND GIRLFRIEND?
AND YOU COULD BE MY NEW YORK GIRLFRIEND
FOR REAL? I'VE NEVER ACTUALLY... HAD A GIRL-FRIEND.
OH, I'M SURE I'LL BE THE FIRST OF MANY!
WANNA TAKE THE MIXTAPE FOR A SPIN?

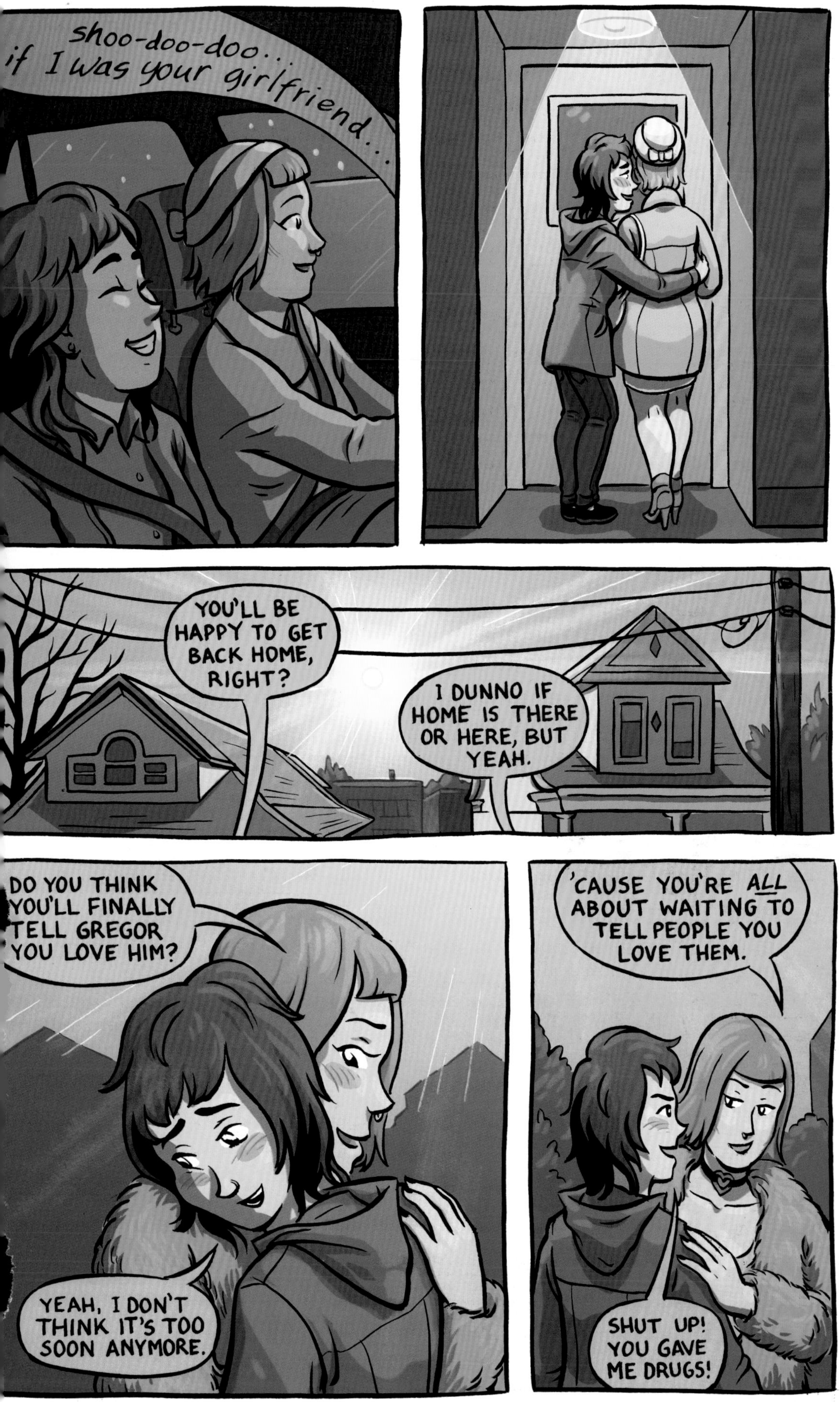
shoo-doo-doo... if I was your girlfriend...
YOU'LL BE HAPPY TO GET BACK HOME, RIGHT?
I DUNNO IF HOME IS THERE OR HERE, BUT YEAH.
DO YOU THINK YOU'LL FINALLY TELL GREGOR YOU LOVE HIM?
YEAH, I DON'T THINK IT'S TOO SOON ANYMORE.
'CAUSE YOU'RE ALL ABOUT WAITING TO TELL PEOPLE YOU LOVE THEM.
SHUT UP! YOU GAVE ME DRUGS!

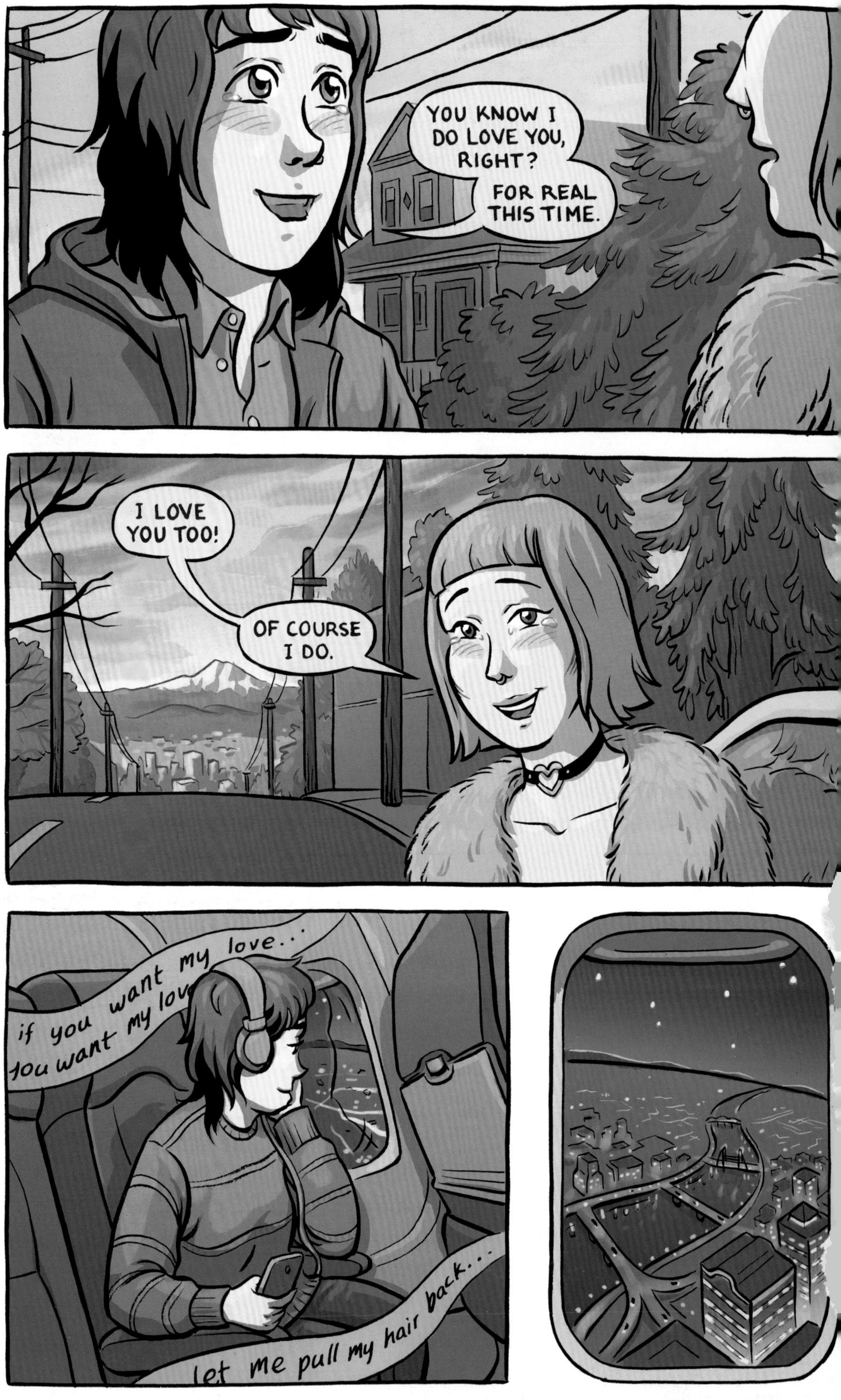
YOU KNOW I DO LOVE YOU, RIGHT?
FOR REAL THIS TIME.
I LOVE YOU TOO!
OF COURSE I DO.
if you want my love...
you want my lov
let me pull my hair back...